Disclaimer

You are ultimately responsible for the success or failure of your crowdfunding campaign, project and/or business and all decisions pertaining to the planning, execution and fulfillment of obligations related to your crowdfunding and business endeavors are solely your responsibility. This publication is based on compiled best practices, research and experience. The author makes no guarantee that your crowdfunding campaign, business or any other endeavor will be successful, but hopes that you will utilize this information to aid in your own success.

Table of Contents

About the Author

"My mission is to help others achieve financial independence and alleviate poverty by providing entrepreneurs with the knowledge, tools, and resources to access capital for their business endeavors."

- Lance McNeill, author of The Comprehensive Crowdfunding Guide®

Lance McNeill is driven by his desire to coach and guide small business owners and aspiring entrepreneurs. In his role of seeing clients through the development process from an idea to successful launch, he looks to crowdfunding as the platform for empowering his clients to take the success of their businesses to the next level. As such, McNeill pioneered the Keep Austin Funded crowdfunding program with local Austin non-profit, Business and Community Lenders of Texas. The Keep Austin Funded program provides technical assistance to those seeking to raise funds through crowdfunding. The program navigates entrepreneurs through both the start-up and crowdfunding processes with an innovative combination of 1-on-1 business coaching and crowdfunding. At the helm of this program, McNeill recognizes crowdfunding as a revolutionary opportunity for start-up entrepreneurs seeking access to capital.

Formerly a business coach in Peace Corps Africa, McNeill brings a unique perspective to entrepreneurship at a global level. An interest in socioeconomics lead McNeill to the AmeriCorps VISTA program, where he helped start a small business coaching program for underserved populations. The program works to empower these families with the tools required to succeed and become financially independent.

McNeill's experience and commitment to helping budding entrepreneurs lead him to writing his debut book titled The Comprehensive Crowdfunding Guide®, a tool to help not only his clients, but an audience at large finding themselves turning to innovative avenues, such as crowdfunding, for capital.

McNeill holds an MBA from the McCoy School of Business at Texas State. As a believer in lifelong learning, he is currently pursuing a second Master's degree at the University of Texas' LBJ School of Public Affairs.

Acknowledgements

Behind any successful project you'll find close friends and family that were supportive from the beginning. Thank you to my best friends, Michael Moore and Christie Wright.

I'd also like to thank June Walker for contributing her list of 100+ common business expenses. Her tax advice, tools and resources for independent professionals are extremely useful. This guide was made possible by the efforts of several other people I wouldn't have otherwise been able to reach if it weren't for crowdsourcing.

Crowdsourced contributors:

Hasinur (Mahib) Rahman of Bangladesh – Book cover designer (http://fiverr.com/hrmahib1994)

Heather Hummel of Charlottesville, Virginia – Bio author (http://fiverr.com/heatherhummel)

Sebastian Jacob of Bangalore, India – Infographic designer (http://fiverr.com/summergraphics)

Thomas Wong, U.S – Infographic designer (http://www.inkvis.com/)

John – Infographic Designer (https://www.fiverr.com/graphicex)

Introduction

When Lizz walked into my office in the fall of 2012, with her business plan in hand, I could tell she was a bit apprehensive about our meeting. She hadn't shared her idea with anyone outside her circle of close friends and family, but she was ready to take that difficult step of moving from concept to implementation.

The City of Austin provides some amazing resources to small business owners and aspiring entrepreneurs, including free (prepaid with tax dollars) and confidential one-on-one coaching through their Small Business Development Program (SBDP). As part of a contract with the City, Business and Community Lenders (BCL) of Texas, a 501©3 nonprofit economic development organization, provided that one-on-one consultation. As the lead coach with BCL, I provided technical assistance on everything from navigating the nuts and bolts of the start-up process (registration, permits, taxes, etc.) to determining financial readiness to apply for a small business loan. Lizz and I met through this program.

When she handed me her business plan, I read the title on the cover page "Gypsy Heart Wandering Photo Booths". I thumbed through the plan until I came across a blueprint drawing of what appeared to be a photo booth attached to the back of a bicycle. I looked over the drawings in detail as she explained her business model, "Gypsy Heart Wandering Photo Booths is a fun mobile photo booth that can be easily transported around Austin's downtown hotspots and year-round festivals". Lizz looked up at me waiting for me to scoff at the quirky idea. I hadn't seen anything like it before, but growing up in Austin, I understood how this business could work and make money. I noticed she relaxed a bit when I told her that I thought the idea was actually very innovative. "So," I asked, "how much is it going to cost to build this Wandering Photo Booth?" "About $6,000," she said.

> ## Crowdfunding
>
> *Crowdfunding is the term used to describe the transparent method of online fundraising whereby funds are pooled from individual contributors to help achieve a defined initiative. It is a democratizing financial frontier that creates opportunities for entrepreneurs to access capital for their endeavors through the collective effort of early adopters and loyal supporters.*

For various reasons, Lizz wasn't an ideal candidate for a loan from BCL and as I began to list off the barriers she would have to overcome to qualify for a loan, she politely interrupted me, "I'm actually interested in crowdfunding. Can you all help with that?" This was 2012 and crowdfunding was just beginning to build buzz. I was familiar with the concept, but didn't know anything about the mechanics. I told Lizz I'd be happy to help in any way I could, but that really we'd be learning about how to manage a crowdfunding campaign together.

We started by piecing together a rough campaign plan and after a couple of weeks launched on Indiegogo. In just over 30 days, Lizz was able to raise the $6,400 she needed to build the Wandering

Photo Booth. Crowdfunding allowed Lizz to take a novel idea and test its validity with early adopters and loyal supporters. I'd love to tell you that Gypsy Heart Photo Booths has been successful and scaled beyond just Austin, but that's not the case. Successfully crowdfunding a new project can bring a lot of advantages and create positive momentum, but it isn't a guarantee for long-term business success and most start-ups go out of business within 5 years. However, Lizz inspired me to learn as much as I could about crowdfunding and put together this Guide so that I could help others pursue their dreams.

This guide is designed to help you plan and execute a successful perks/rewards-based crowdfunding campaign. It is a compilation based on research, statistics, best practices and my experience as a small business coach. I hope it will provide ideas, advice and inspiration for whatever endeavor you embark on. Perks/rewards-based crowdfunding is the offering of goods, services and/or creative gratitude in exchange for financial contributions from family, friends, supporters and early adopters. These contributions provide the validation of your proposed project or endeavor.

Other forms of crowdfunding include donation-based crowdfunding, peer-to-peer lending, crowdfund investing, and royalty or revenue-based crowdfunding.

Donation-based crowdfunding is typically used by non-profits without the promise of any perk or reward in exchange for money. This is basically traditional philanthropy with crowdfunding as the conduit for fundraising. However, there is nothing stopping non-profits from using a combination of donation and perks/rewards-based crowdfunding.

It's important to note that in order to accept tax exempt donations, you must be a tax exempt entity, the most common being a 501©3 charitable non-profit. If you're accepting contributions for a personal cause, then really you're asking for a gift, not a donation. I'm generally skeptical of crowdfunding being used to fund personal causes, so I don't mention it in this Guide. However, many of the fundamentals outlined throughout this book are also applicable to personal cause or gift-based crowdfunding.

I frequently see crowdfunding campaigns ask for donations and maybe it's my background in nonprofits, but I tend to cringe every time I see 'donation' associated with any fundraising effort not related to a 501©3 nonprofit organization. It might seem like a trivial difference in wording, but the perceptions you create about your project are very important. Why would I donate to a musician? Musicians are not charitable organizations with tax-exemption. Musicians are artists with something of value to offer in exchange for my contribution. So, unless you're truly a charitable organization, use words like "back, contribute, fund, support" and avoid the word "donate".

Another type of crowdfunding is Crowdfund investing or CFI. CFI allows ownership or equity in a company to be offered in exchange for financial contributions. This method of crowdfunding was legalized in the United States with the passage of the Jumpstart Our Business Start-ups (JOBS) Act, which was signed into law in April of 2012. The Act promises to break down many of the outdated hurdles to funding faced by entrepreneurs in the early stages of business. Unfortunately, the SEC has held back the most groundbreaking components of crowdfund investing, as it struggles to create fair and balanced regulations that protect investors while at the same time staying true to the purpose of the JOBS Act. At the time of this writing, the SEC has been sorting these considerations out since the initial legislation was passed.

Crowdfunding is also being used to disrupt lending. Peer-to-peer lending is the collection of many micro-loans to form one single loan and royalty crowdfunding promises a share of revenue from a project in exchange for funding. CFI, peer-to-peer lending and royalty-based crowdfunding will not be covered in this edition of the guide, although some of the advice given for donation and perk/reward-based crowdfunding might still be useful in those pursuits. However, there are many technical and legal details that accompany some of the other forms of crowdfunding, so please do your research beforehand. This guide is designed to walk you step-by-step through a donation or perks/rewards-based campaign.

I'm inspired by the promise of crowdfunding as a revolutionary tool to help bring better access to capital to small business owners, non-profits, social entrepreneurs and anyone bold enough to turn their dreams into a reality. Crowdfunding isn't just a new frontier in fundraising or finance, it's the future of a much stronger and truer democracy. Beyond fundraising, crowdfunding has created one of the best methods of obtaining proof of concept and reaching early adopters, loyal customers and lifelong supporters.

Figure 1: An American Committee Fundraising statuette; Source: National Park Service, Statue of Liberty

Crowdfunding may have become a popular buzzword, but it is certainly not a new concept. In fact, one of the earliest and most inspiring examples of crowdfunding stands proudly on Liberty Island as a beacon of freedom and democracy for the entire world to admire. The Statue of Liberty Enlightening the World or just the Statue of Liberty for short, cost approximately $250,000 to build (in 1880 dollars) and was paid for by the French people - not the French government - through a creative fundraising effort that we recognize today as crowdfunding[1]. The Statue of Liberty's sculptor, Auguste Bartholdi, created some of the first known crowdfunding rewards when he produced 6" and 12" Lady Liberty statuettes and engraved contributors' names on the bottom[2]. The 6" statuette sold for $1 and the 12" statuette sold for $5. The figure to the right is one of the original statuettes available for viewing at the Statue of Liberty National Monument Park.

---

[1] Liberty Island Chronology. U.S National Park Service. Statue of Liberty. <http://www.nps.gov/stli/historyculture/liberty-island-a-chronology.htm>

[2] McNamara, Robert. Who Paid for the Statue of Liberty? 19th Century History. About.com. Accessed 3 December 2013 <http://history1800s.about.com/od/immigration/f/statuelibertypaid.htm>

Through their grassroots effort, the French people raised enough funds to build the actual statue, but it was the United States' responsibility to contribute funds for the platform that Lady Liberty stands on today. The 1880s were still a difficult time for our country and after a prolonged Civil War and Reconstruction, Uncle Sam's purse strings were still pulled tightly. A little more than halfway through the construction of the platform, funding dried up and the entire project stood on the brink of failure.

The picture to the right shows the pedestal under construction[3].

A federal bill to fund the $100,000 needed to complete the construction of the pedestal failed to pass appropriations. A separate initiative put forth by New York's state government to fund the project up to $50,000 passed the legislative branch, but was vetoed by then Governor, Grover Cleveland. Just when it looked like Lady Liberty would be spending the rest of her days in France, Joseph Pulitzer stepped up with a solution.

Figure 2: Pedestal for Bartholdi's Statue of Liberty

Figure 3: PULITZER, JOSEPH. Chromolithograph

Joseph Pulitzer[4], best known today as the namesake for the Pulitzer Prize, decided to appeal directly to U.S citizens to fund the remaining project costs[5]. He used his newspaper, *The World*, to reach citizens in mass

"We must raise the money! The World is the people's paper, and now it appeals to the people to come forward and raise the money. The $250,000 that the making of the Statue cost was paid in by the masses of the French people- by the working men, the tradesmen, the shop girls, the artisans- by all, irrespective of class or condition. Let us respond in like manner. Let us not wait for the millionaires to give us this money. It is not a gift from the millionaires of France to

[3] Snyder, W.P. Pedestal for Bartholdi's Statue of Liberty on Bedloe's Island, New York Harbor. Harper's Weekly, Volume XXIX, No. 1485, 6 June 1885, Page 356. Accessed 3 Dec, 2013. <http://commons.wikimedia.org/wiki/File:HARPER%27S_WEEKLY-NewYork_6_June_1885.jpg>
[4] PULITZER, JOSEPH. Chromolithograph. [Ca. 1904.]. U.S Library of Congress. **Location:** LOT 10489 **Reproduction Number:** LC-USZ62-49254 **Note:** Gift, Ralph Pulitzer, 1966. Accessed 3 Dec, 2013 <http://upload.wikimedia.org/wikipedia/commons/2/27/Pulitzer.jpg>
[5] http://www.pulitzer.org/historyofprizes

the millionaires of America, but a gift of the whole people of France to the whole people of America.[6]"

This direct appeal led to a sixth month "campaign" with 125,000 people contributing a combined $100,000. The funds raised were enough to complete the construction of the platform. Mr. Pulitzer led by example, contributing $250 of his own funds[7]. The average contribution was only 80 cents per contributor – truly a grassroots effort. In recognition of citizens' generous contributions, Pulitzer published the names of the 125,000 Statue of Liberty "backers" in his newspaper[8]. This kind of recognition as a reward is still popular in many successful crowdfunding campaigns today. I share this story to highlight the democratizing power and potential of crowdfunding and crowdsourcing innovations.

Online crowdfunding has become a groundbreaking new financial frontier that creates opportunities for entrepreneurs, artists, do-gooders, and anyone looking to access capital for their projects. Almost anything imaginable is possible without the barriers of traditional capital loans or investment. Through social media, online payment processing and the transparency of crowdfunding platforms, we are able to achieve the fundraising success realized by Pulitzer over a 5 ½ month period, in just 4-6 weeks. Crowdfunding is giving people the freedom to fund what they believe in and for that reason, it is not only here to stay, but over time, it is something that will truly strengthen our democracy.

Indeed, it's exciting to see crowdfunding used in support of so many different initiatives, from start-up capital for new businesses, non-profits, social enterprises, etc, to capital in support of an existing businesses' expanding operations. Yet, this new frontier, compounded with the challenges of starting or expanding a business or project, is often overwhelming. In fact, the majority of the projects on even the most popular crowdfunding sites like Kickstarter and Indiegogo, fail to raise their funding goals, with success rates of approximately 45%[9] or less.

My hope is that the best practices and research presented in this guide will increase your chances of success. Not every piece of advice in this guide will be applicable to your project, but the majority of this information should help you think about things you might have overlooked. As you embark on your crowdfunding campaign, and ultimately the project you're raising funds for, I wish you all the best.

Sincerely,

Lance McNeill, MBA

---

[6] http://www.nps.gov/stli/historyculture/joseph-pulitzer.htm
[7] Brian, Denis. Pulitzer: A Life. 2001. Pg 104
[8] http://www.nps.gov/stli/historyculture/joseph-pulitzer.htm
[9] Mollick, Ethan. The Dynamics of Crowdfunding: Determinants of Success and Failure. Jul 25. 2012. The Wharton School of the University of Pennsylvania.

Crowdfunding Campaign Checklist

As you work through this guide, come back to this checklist and mark off tasks that you've completed.

- ☐ I'm mentally prepared and have realistic expectations for crowdfunding
    - ☐ I have a written mission and SMART goals for this project
    - ☐ I'm willing to ask others to contribute their time, influence and money to this project.
    - ☐ There is nothing going on in my personal life that will distract me from planning and executing a successful campaign.
    - ☐ I have spoken to my family and close friends about my plans to launch a crowdfunding campaign.
    - ☐ I have 50-60 hours to plan my crowdfunding campaign before it launches
    - ☐ I have 80-120 hours available to devote to executing the crowdfunding campaign.

- ☐ Determine project costs
    - ☐ Itemize your project costs in a spreadsheet (project cost template available in appendix)
    - ☐ Include estimated success and credit card processing fees in my total costs
    - ☐ Include the costs of perks and rewards

- ☐ Prepare campaign timeline
    - ☐ Identify and contact individuals that will advocate for this project
    - ☐ Identify holidays, observances and events that will take place during the crowdfunding campaign.
    - ☐ Create a crowdfunding campaign calendar

- ☐ Establish and enhance your online presence
    - ☐ Obtain domain name and build website (if applicable)
    - ☐ Create a Facebook page (personal and/or business)
    - ☐ Join LinkedIn
    - ☐ Join relevant Meet-up groups
    - ☐ Join twitter
    - ☐ Start a blog (if applicable)
    - ☐ Identify relevant bloggers and influencers in the community or industry
    - ☐ Identify other relevant media outlets in your community or industry
    - ☐ Complete the Social Network REV Assessment

- ☐ Develop exciting perks and rewards
    - ☐ Offer the product or service as a reward
    - ☐ Conduct market research with perks/rewards
    - ☐ Partner with a non-profit, church or other community organization
    - ☐ Research successful campaigns related to your project for perk/reward ideas
    - ☐ Create a special perk/reward that will be introduced after the campaign launches
    - ☐ Create perks/rewards that align with popular holidays or observances that occur during your crowdfunding campaign.

- ☐ Create perks/rewards that can be fulfilled or delivered within a reasonable timeframe.
- ☐ Offer perks/rewards at appropriate tiers and intervals
- ☐ Complete the Perks/Rewards Worksheet

☐ Produce an effective video pitch
- ☐ Determine if you will produce the video yourself or find a videographer to assist.
- ☐ Create your video storyboard
- ☐ Tell a great story
- ☐ Video is less than 3 minutes long
- ☐ Upload video to YouTube or Vimeo

☐ Conduct research and choose the right crowdfunding platform

☐ REV up your network
- ☐ Establish social proof for your crowdfunding campaign.
- ☐ Share updates and progress reports about the campaign
- ☐ Identify connections that will share your posts, tweets, updates, etc.

☐ Fulfill your perk/reward obligations
- ☐ Thank your backers and set realistic expectations for them going forward.
- ☐ Share your story and keep the buzz going

Mental Preparation and Realistic Expectations

Before you even start thinking about crowdfunding you need to consider a few important questions. These questions may seem obvious, but I've witnessed entrepreneurs fail in their fundraising endeavors because they weren't honest with themselves from the beginning. If you're unable to answer yes to the following questions, then I recommend you set this guide aside and put your crowdfunding aspirations on hold until you can.

1. Why are you raising funds?

Your project should have a clearly defined scope – a beginning and an end. Crowdfunding is not about perpetual fundraising and therefore, you should be able to convey to the crowd how the funds will help make measurable progress toward the project's goals.

A good example is raising $5,000 to place an initial order for 100 units to begin to build an inventory and fulfill initial purchase orders or raising $30,000 to build a community playground. It's very clear how funds will be used and how they will help achieve measurable goals.

Those who contribute to a project fundraising for to build a new playground know when the project is successful because they will be able to see the playground being built and eventually completed. On the other hand, raising funds to support you, personally, as you spend time conducting research and development for a product prototype is not a good reason to seek funds from the crowd.

The crowd is more likely to support your project if they believe the majority of their contribution will go toward achieving something measurable and tangible.

2. Do you have a clear mission and goals for your project?

This question builds off of the previous one and will help you define the scope of your project.

Yes

Great, now make sure they're in writing. A goal is just a dream until you've written it down on paper. These two items are a key component to any project proposal, strategy or business plan.

No

I strongly recommend you have at least a rough draft of a project proposal or strategic plan before thinking about fundraising. This might be a marketing plan, a business plan, canvas or simply a project outline. I've included a mission statement and goal setting worksheet in the appendix to help with the mechanics of creating a mission statement and goals.

Helpful resource: Mission Statement Worksheet (located in the appendix)

Helpful resource: SMART Goals Worksheet (located in the appendix)

3. **Can you count on your friends and family to support you in your endeavor?**

Yes

Good, because you're really going to need them during this process. If you haven't already, start talking with friends and family as soon as possible about what you're trying to accomplish. See if you can get a sense of their willingness to support you in this endeavor. Mention to them that you're thinking about crowdfunding and see what they say. Let them know it's a  lot of work and you'd need as much help as possible. Later sections will guide you on how to ask more specifically for their help and as you read, you'll gain a better understanding of what exactly you might need the most help with, but mentioning your plans now will plant the seed for later on.

No

Planning and executing a successful crowdfunding campaign takes a lot of work – way too much for just one person. If you cannot count on the support of your friends and family, then crowdfunding successfully will be very difficult.

4. **Are you willing and bold enough to ask others to contribute time, influence and money to your project?**

Yes

Excellent! You must believe in your project enough to be able to ask, confidently, for others' support. If you're an introvert and independent minded, like me, selling something and asking for contributions may not come natural. It will take work to overcome your reservations, but if you believe in your project's mission and its value to others, you can be assured that your hard work is selfless and part of a greater goal.

No

If you are unwilling to ask for contributions for your project, then crowdfunding is not for you. If you're an independent minded person, like me, then you might be hesitant to ask other people for help. If you're unable or unwilling to overcome that hesitation then you might consider bootstrapping your project - paying for expenses from other sources of earned income or savings. There is an art to asking and this guide will help you explore that art, but you must be willing to ask.

If you're still hesitant, I recommend you watch an incredible TED talk by Amanda Palmer on the art of asking: http://www.ted.com/talks/amanda_palmer_the_art_of_asking.html

Amanda Palmer is a very successful Rock Musician who has leveraged the power of the crowd to establish a new kind of relationship with her fans. If Amanda's TED talk still doesn't change your mind about making the "ask," then you need to find other sources of funding for your project.

Crowdfunding Myth:
"Crowdfunding is simply a form of panhandling". Crowdfunding, in fact, is not panhandling. A panhandler is a beggar in the streets asking for money. Those that use crowdfunding to fund a personal cause, especially when it's not an urgent life-threatening need, are crowdfunding at a cost – they're expending their social capital and it will be more difficult for them to return to the crowd and ask for funds in the future. This is one reason I'm skeptical of crowdfunding for personal causes unless I personally know the person in need. Crowdfunding for perks and rewards, on the other

hand, is offering something of value in exchange for a financial contribution. It is a two-way exchange.

5. **Is anything going on in your personal life that might distract or deter you from planning and executing a successful crowdfunding campaign?**

Yes or unsure

I spent about three or four weeks working with an entrepreneur in the retail industry to plan a crowdfunding campaign for her new product line and manufacturing initial inventory. We had made considerable progress and were excited about the upcoming launch when she found out that her mother had just been diagnosed with cancer. We discussed whether or not to move forward with planning and launch, but ultimately we determined that it was best to postpone the crowdfunding campaign for the time being.

It goes without saying that you know yourself better than anyone else, but take a serious moment to reflect on anything going on in your personal life that deserves your immediate attention. You can still achieve quite a bit working through this guide and the campaign planning process until you're absolutely ready to launch.

No

Skip to the next section and let's get started.

Notes:

_____

_____

_____

_____

_____

_____

_____

Product: Lightweight child carrier
Amount raised: $31,752
Campaign duration: 60 days
Crowdfunding platform: Indiegogo

The Freeloader child carrier is the brainchild of two fathers from Austin, Texas who enjoy spending time with their family, especially while travelling and exploring the outdoors. As many parents will testify, about midway through a long day sightseeing or hiking, children start to run out of energy and need to be carried. The Freeloader provides a durable, light-weight solution for parents looking to enjoy the entire day with their family without breaking their back.

Nathan, The Freeloader's co-founder, was kind enough to sit down with me and share some lessons he learned during his crowdfunding campaign. He was able to raise more than $31,000 over a 60 day period. Think about his advice as you work through this guide.

Q: Did you have any reservations about asking friends, family and strangers for funds?

A: *"I strongly believe that The Freeloader is a product that benefits families and that makes asking easier. With that said, I do wish that I would have discussed my plans to crowdfund with my close friends and family sooner and well before I asked for their time or contributions."*

Q: How much of the $31,752 came from close friends and family?

A: *"About $8,000" (25%)*

Q: What role did your friends and family play besides their financial contributions?

A: *"I had about 10 people I called and another 10 that I emailed for help with various things throughout the campaign; everything from forwarding emails to helping with social media. This is why I say it's so important to involve your close friends and family as early on as possible because they are the people who can help take you that extra mile."*

Q: How many hours per week did you work on the campaign?

A: *"Probably around 20-30 hours"*

Q: Looking back, what stands out as a really good decision you made?

A: *"We hired a local PR firm to help us with our press release and to connect us with relevant media outlets. We didn't have a huge budget, but they worked with us and exceeded our expectations. They really made a difference in our campaign. One piece of advice though - give them plenty of notice, at least 3-4 weeks before you launch your campaign."*

Q: If you could go back, what would you do differently?

A: *"During the campaign, I was so focused on contributions that I ignored the actual costs of shipping and handling. I received contributions from around the world and I included a small upcharge for the added costs. However, I underestimated those costs considerably. If I could go back, I would have researched the actual costs and forced myself to include that into the price."*

Q: What general advice do you have for those thinking about a crowdfunding campaign?

A: *"Don't underestimate the amount of time and work that goes into planning and executing a campaign. Set realistic expectations and don't assume that your campaign is going to go viral – that's like believing you're actually going to win the lottery. You're going to have to reach out to people directly, you can't just post general updates on social media. Out of 600+ Facebook friends, I took time to reach out to about half with a personal message. It takes that level of time and effort to be successful."*

Determine Your Project Costs

How much should I seek to raise through perks/rewards based crowdfunding? This is a question I hear frequently, but the better way to think about the question is to ask "what financial resources are needed to achieve the project goals and will perks/rewards based crowdfunding be appropriate for the entire amount needed?" If it isn't, crowdfunding might be a significant part of a larger funding strategy that should be explored more thoroughly before launching a campaign.

This section helps you determine how much you need to raise for your project and assess whether or not that is a realistic amount to fundraise exclusively with perks/rewards based crowdfunding or if you will need additional financing to fill the gap.

Determine Your Project Costs

What financial resources do you need to achieve your project goals and will perks/rewards based crowdfunding be appropriate for the entire amount I need to raise? Answer the questions below to get started on the first steps of your crowdfunding campaign planning process.

1 Do you know how much money is needed to accomplish your project goals?

If you know your total project costs and have an itemized list of estimates or quotes, continue to question 2. If you don't, use the Project Cost Worksheet and list of common business expenses included in the appendix.

2 Have you included the estimated success and credit card processing fees in your projected costs?

Most crowdfunding platforms take a success fee, which is a small percentage of the total amount successfully raised. In addition, credit card processing fees are approximately 3%. Make sure to include these fees in your project costs.

3 Have you included the cost of your perks and rewards?

Keep in mind that it may cost money to purchase, package, and ship some of your perks/rewards. Later sections delve more deeply into these considerations.

4 Does your total project sum to less than $35,000?

90% of perk/rewards-based projects raise < $10,000. If you plan to raise > $35,000, be sure you have the network connections, PR support and unique value proposition needed to achieve that goal.

5 Can your 1st level networks (family, close friends, colleagues) support approximately 25%-33% of your total project costs?

If so, then you're seeking a realistic amount to raise with perks/rewards-based crowdfunding and your chances of success will be much greater.

Crowdfunding Myth:

"I'm going to raise $100K through crowdfunding"! You've probably heard about a few crowdfunding projects that raised $50K, $100K or even a million dollars. What you probably didn't realize is that only 1.1% of all crowdfunding campaigns successfully raised more than $100K[10]. That means 98.9% of all crowdfunding campaigns raised less than $100K, so it's possible, but the odds are not in your favor.

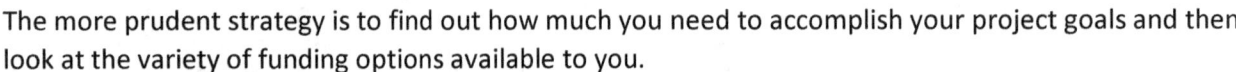

Unsuccessful campaigns that never reach their goal	57.27%
Successful campaigns that raised $10K or less	36%
Successful campaigns that raised $10K-$19,999	6.7%
Successful campaigns that raised $20K-$99,999	5.5%
Successful campaigns that raised $100K or more	1.1%

The more prudent strategy is to find out how much you need to accomplish your project goals and then look at the variety of funding options available to you.

1. Do you know how much money is needed to accomplish your project goals?

Yes

If you know your total project's costs and have an itemized list of estimates or quotes, continue to question 2. If you haven't yet itemized your project costs, it's likely that you have a ballpark estimate, but not a true project cost projection. We recommend you use the Project Cost Worksheet along with the list of common business expenses included in the appendix to make sure you haven't overlooked anything.

It's easy to come up with a ballpark estimate for your project costs, but often that methodology leads to underestimated projections. If you come up short on the funding side because you underestimated your costs, it's much more difficult at that point to go back and seek additional funding. It's better to estimate as accurately as possible during the planning stage and include a cushion for the miscellaneous or unexpected. There are fewer issues with coming in under budget than going over.

No

If you're still unsure how much you need to raise for your endeavor then you're not yet ready to plan your crowdfunding campaign. A simple estimate or ballpark figure might suffice while you're still in the idea stage, but you'll need more than that when it's time to seek funding. We recommend you research what costs are involved with your project by getting actual estimates or quotes, itemize those costs in a spreadsheet (see project cost template in the appendix) and sum the total. It's also a good idea to cite the source where the quote or estimate came from so you can defend it against anyone who might challenge your projections. The Project Cost Template and list of common business expenses include many common project costs to help you start brainstorming.

Helpful resource: Project Cost Template (located in the appendix)

Helpful resource: June Walker's list of 100+ Common Business Expenses (located in the appendix)

---

[10] Kickstarter 2014. Statista 2014.

2. **Have you included the estimated success and credit card processing fees in your projected costs?**

Most crowdfunding platforms take a success fee, which is a small percentage of the total amount successfully raised. Most platforms will charge a success fee at the end of the campaign, instead of taking fees up-front. In addition to the success fee, credit card processing fees are approximately 3%.

Yes

Make sure you've followed the logic outlined in the example below.

No

You need to include the platform's success fees and credit card processing fees in your project costs. For example, if you know you need $10,000 for your project and the platform's success fees = 5%, then you need to add in those fees + 3% for credit card processing fees. In addition, it's best to add in approximately 1% in addition to those fees to account for the increased fees on the overall increased project costs.

For example, let's say you want to raise $10,000 for your project. You need to include an additional $500 for the 5% success fee charged by the platform and $300 for the 3% credit card processing fees. Now the total amount you're seeking to raise is $10,800, right? Close, but not quite. If the platform and credit card companies are taking a total of 8% of $10,800 that only leaves you with $9,936, which is $64 short of your goal. This happens because the total project amount increased and the net fees also increased. When you add in an additional 1%, you ensure that you've covered the net fees and it makes for easy math. So, 9% added to the $10,000 project = $10,900. When you subtract 8% from that total raise, you're left with $10,028!

So, to summarize, in this example we would incorporate the additional fees using the following calculation:

Example:

$10,000 *(1 + .09) = $10,900 = total project costs including fees
$10,900 * .92 = $10,028 = total earned from crowdfunding after fees

If you're unsure of the platform's fees, please reference the section on choosing the right platform in later in this guide and then double check on the crowdfunding platform's website. The fees are normally hidden in the FAQs.

3. Have you included the cost of your perks and rewards?

At this stage, you may not have an idea of what you'll offer as a perk/reward in exchange for contributions. Later sections delve more deeply into how to develop exciting perks and rewards, but as you calculate your project costs you need to keep in mind that it may cost money to purchase, package and ship some of those perks and rewards. This is especially important if you are going to ship anything overseas.

Yes

Excellent! You're well ahead of the curve since you've already got your perks and rewards in mind. If they change, make sure you go back and update your total project costs to include the cost of your perks and rewards + any packaging or shipping costs.

No

That's okay, we'll look at perks and rewards in greater detail later on in the guide. Once you've determined your perks and rewards, we'll walk you through adding their costs into your total project expenditures. Continue with the checklist, but just keep in mind that the cost of perks + packaging and shipping should be factored into your total project costs. The U.S Postal Service website offers a decent calculator for figuring international and domestic shipping costs:

Helpful Resource: USPS Postage Price Calculator (http://ircalc.usps.gov/)

4. Does your total project sum to less than $35,000?

Yes

How much will your total project cost? _____

Continue to the next question.

No

90% of successful non-equity or perks/rewards-based crowdfunding projects raise less than $10,000.[11] That means that most successful projects that successfully raise more than $30,000-$35,000 are significant outliers and should not be considered a typical perk/reward-based campaign raise.

If you plan to raise more than $30,000-$35,000 through perk/reward based crowdfunding, be sure you have the network connections, public relations contacts and a unique value proposition to support such an ask. Alternatively, you might look to other financing options to complete the fundraising puzzle.

---

[11] Massolution 2012 Crowdfunding Industry Report. Crowdsourcing.org < http://www.crowdsourcing.org/research>

For example, you might use crowdfunding to acquire the minimum 15%-20% equity injection that traditional lenders require to qualify your project for a loan. If you're able to approach a lender with the funds you've raised from a successful crowdfunding campaign, then you'll be in a much stronger position as a loan applicant.

The same can be said when approaching a private investor. Anytime you can bring your own funds to a project, you will make a more compelling case to investors and lenders. The more cash or equity injection you can bring, the better. If you don't personally have the funds to contribute, then bringing the crowd's funds is just as good, if not better. You're not only bringing funds from the crowd, you're also bringing the validation of these early adopters as proof of concept.

Alternatively, you might also consider scaling down the project or breaking it up into multiple phases of growth. For example, if you're an author of a crowdfunding book, you could crowdfund just the first 1-2 chapters and come back to crowdfund the rest in a second campaign.

The Gourmet by Numbers Case Study

Heather is the founder and CEO of Gourmet by Numbers, which offers ready-to-cook meal kits. Gourmet by Numbers cuts out the shopping and chopping hassle, making it possible to have a gourmet meal cooked and ready to eat in 30 minutes or less.

Gourmet by Numbers' start-up costs were estimated at approximately $200,000, including the lease and build-out of a commercial kitchen space needed to prepare the meal kits[12]. Heather's equity injection wasn't sufficient for all of the start-up costs, so she sought to fill her funding gap with crowdfunding and/or a loan.

Start-ups are risky, but food or restaurant related start-ups are perceived by many lenders to be even riskier because of their relatively high failure rate. Even if a potential borrower has great credit, sufficient collateral and meets all the objective requirements for a loan, many lenders will still balk at a restaurant related start-

> **Equity injection**
>
> *An infusion of cash or capital into the business by the business owner(s). This infusion of cash or capital into the business increases the owners' equity. For example, if a total project costs $100,000 and the owner(s) contribute $25,000, they've contributed a 25% equity injection.*

up. When Heather came to Business and Community Lenders of Texas, a nonprofit 501©3 small business lender, those same concerns were discussed.

However, Heather was willing to diversify her sources of start-up funding by using crowdfunding. She raised $22,810 on Indiegogo and closed a considerable portion of her funding gap. Not only did she obtain additional funding, she also validated Gourmet by Numbers by identifying her early adopters and loyal customers. Objectively, the $22,810 did make the deal stronger from the lender's perspective, but subjectively, the identification and capture of early adopters and loyal customers to help prove the

---

[12] For purposes of confidentiality, the numbers in this case study have been changed.

concept was just as valuable. Gourmet by Numbers is up and running because of the creativity used to finance and fund their start-up expenses.

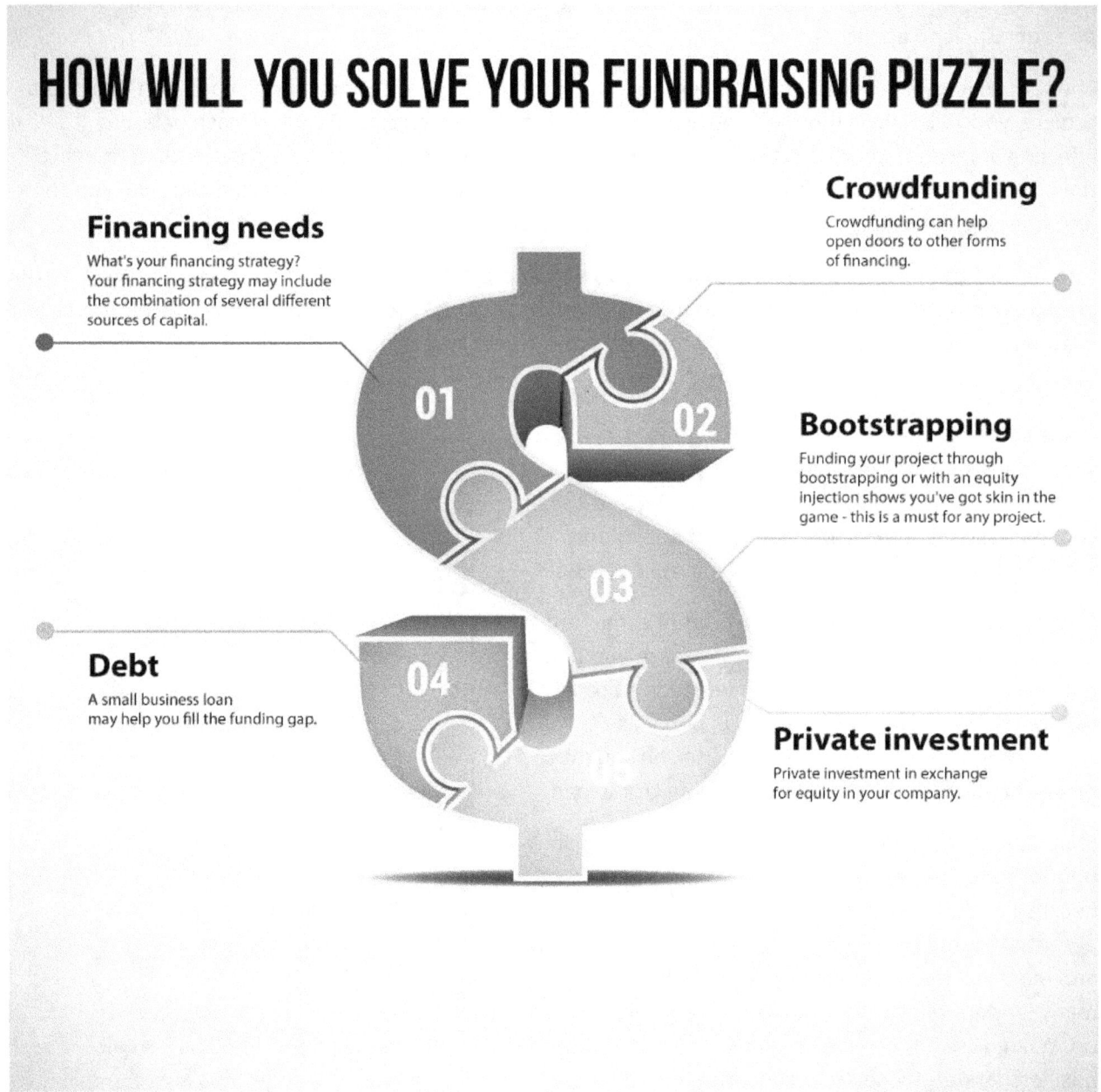

5. **Can your 1st level network (family and close friends or colleagues) support approximately 25%-33% of your total project costs?**

Your 1st level network is comprised of your family and closest friends. These are the people who contribute because they love you and will do anything in their power to see you succeed. For these people, the details of the project might be a secondary consideration in whether or not they contribute; first and foremost they are contributing because this is your project.

Yes

Great! If you're certain that your 1ˢᵗ level network, which is usually comprised of family, close friends and colleagues, can contribute approximately 25%-33% of the total project amount, then you're seeking a realistic amount to raise with perks/rewards-based crowdfunding. Skip ahead to the next question.

Unsure

If you're unsure whether or not your 1ˢᵗ level network, comprised of family, close friends and colleagues, can contribute approximately 25%-33% of the total project amount, utilize the Network REV Assessment Tool™ in the appendix to help you make that determination.

You can also ask them if they're willing and able to contribute to your campaign. I admit this is easier said than done, but remember, in order to be successful with crowdfunding you need to be bold enough to ask for funds.

No

If you do not believe that your 1ˢᵗ level network, comprised of family, close friends and colleagues, can contribute approximately 25%-33% of the total project amount, then you might be seeking an unrealistic amount for perks/rewards based crowdfunding.

One option you might consider is to scale down the project to the point that your first level network is able to support approximately 25%-33% of the total project amount. Utilize the Network REV Assessment Tool™ in the appendix to help you make that determination.

If you're not able to scale down the project sufficiently, then you should look at other ways to fill the funding gap. Crowdfunding can be utilized in tandem with a private investment and/or a loan. Private investment, crowdfund investing (CFI) and lending are all subjects that fall outside the scope of this checklist.

Helpful Resource: Social Media Network REV Assessment Tool™

6. Does your project offer unique value to your target market?

A project, product or service offering should have unique value that can be defined and differentiated from other similar projects, products and service offerings. That doesn't mean that it has to be a completely new invention, but you should be able to articulate how you're filling a need that no one else is able to do in quite the same way. Some unique value propositions can include geographic exclusivity, new or differentiated features and benefits, lower price, higher quality, etc.

Yes

Excellent! Campaigns with a project, product and/or service that offer unique value, not only compared to other crowdfunding campaigns, but to other products and services in general tend to be more successful and will likely raise more funds on average.

Below, list 1-3 unique value propositions your project, product and/or service offers:

_____

_____

_____

_____

Unsure

If you're unsure what unique value your project, product and/or service offers, then you should focus on the market analysis and marketing strategy sections of your business/strategic plan until you're able to list the unique value your product or service offers customers. Check with your local government's economic development office for available resources to assist you with a market analysis and business/strategic plan.

No

If you're not offering a project, product or service with unique value, it will be difficult to raise funds from the crowd. The crowd contributes because they want to see individuals behind a project succeed in their endeavor, but they're also looking to contribute to something unique, that gives them value and is differentiated or special from other offerings available. You should conduct an environmental scan, a market analysis and tweak your business model until you're able to offer something unique and differentiated. At this time, those are all areas that fall outside the scope of this checklist, but here's a quick example:

Let's say you want to Crowdfund a coffee shop. Most towns and cities already have a coffee shop, so how do you compel the crowd to contribute? Well, maybe the original coffee shop doesn't offer food and you will, maybe they don't have event space and you will, or maybe the community has grown in population recently and another coffee shop is justified purely by demographics. You should be researching what your competitors are doing well and not doing well, find your niche and justify and validate your business with data.

Check with your local government's economic development office for other resources to assist you with an environmental scan, market analysis and strategic business plan.

Notes:

_____

_____

_____

_____

_____

_____

_____

Prepare Your Campaign Timeline

Most crowdfunding campaigns don't require a large financial investment, but they do require a substantial time commitment. In addition to the time investment, it's also critical to consider when to launch a campaign and how long it will run. Answer the questions below to make sure you've prepared a realistic timeline.

1. **Do you have at least 50-60 hours to dedicate toward planning your crowdfunding campaign <u>before you launch</u>?**

Typically, it will take you an estimated 50-60 hours to work through everything in this guide.

Yes

Wonderful! You're on track toward success. Make sure you're budgeting your time, especially if you have a day job or attend school. Skip ahead to the next question.

No

If you need to launch your crowdfunding campaign without 50-60 hours of prep time and you haven't done anything to prepare besides obtain this checklist, then you might be rushing along without adequate time to plan for success. This is especially true for those that are launching a crowdfunding campaign and holding a full-time or part-time job, going to school, etc. I definitely recommend you give yourself at least 50-60 hours lead time before launching your campaign.

2. **Do you know how many days you will run your crowdfunding campaign?**

Yes

 **The crowdfunding campaign will last _____ days.**

Research shows that 30 day campaigns have a relatively higher chance of success[13]. If you are planning to run the campaign for longer, you'll need to focus on strategies that can carry the momentum beyond a standard 30 day campaign. You might also consider the 35-45 day crowdfunding strategy described below.

No or Unsure

If you don't know or you're unsure of how long to run your crowdfunding campaign, consider the 35-45 day crowdfunding campaign strategy outlined below:

---

[13] Mollick, Ethan. The Dynamics of Crowdfunding: Determinants of Success and Failure. Jul 25. 2012. The Wharton School of the University of Pennsylvania.

First 5-10 days	Next 30-35 days
• Encourage just family and friends to contribute	• Announce campaign launch to public and through social media

Run a 35-45 day campaign and use the first 5-10 days to get your first level network to contribute before you announce your campaign to the public or through social media. This gives some extra time for your close friends and family to contribute and provide that critical social proof, which is discussed more extensively in later sections of the guide. By the time you announce your campaign to the public and through social media, you will hopefully already have contributions from friends and family. This strengthens the campaign because it will appear that the campaign has just been announced, but already has contributions rolling in.

3. Do you have 80-120 hours to devote to the execution of a month long campaign?

Yes

Good, because during the campaign you're going to need all that time and more to engage and re-engage your network of supporters and potential backers.

No

If you don't have at least 80-120 hours to devote to a month long crowdfunding campaign, you'll need to lean heavily on a team or individual who can. Close friends, family or a business partner can help you manage your crowdfunding campaign.

Also, Elance.com is a great resource for increasing your capacity. Elance is a crowdsourcing platform that allows you to reach virtual assistants, marketing experts and even experienced crowdfunding campaign managers from around the world.

Helpful Resource: www.elance.com

4. **Do you have an individual or team that is willing to advocate for your project and campaign and can they contribute at least a combined 20-40 hours toward a month long campaign?**

Yes

 Great! List those people below and reach out to them to guarantee their support using a personal message. An email message is fine, but make sure you're addressing them by name and appealing to them on a personal level. Use the email message prompt below to help you get started.

Team Member Advocate	Hours committed

No

You should really look at bringing on at least one individual who can be an advocate for your project and crowdfunding campaign. An advocate or team will increase your capacity to execute a successful campaign by sharing your posts, favoriting your tweets, writing emails, etc. A close friend or family member usually makes for an active advocate. Send them an email and ask them if they would be willing to help. You can use the email message prompt below to get you started.

Also, some crowdfunding platforms, like www.indiegogo.com or www.vovation.com have affiliates or partners that might be able to fill the role of an advocate. These entities are usually local and have a mission to help small businesses and nonprofits start, grow and succeed. If you're unable to recruit an advocate, team or partner organization, then I recommend you reconsider launching a campaign until you've found one, but I'm guessing if you ask someone they will be willing to help.

Dear _____,

I hope this email finds you doing well. I'm writing to let you know that I've decided to pursue my dream of (describe business/non-profit/project here in no more than 1-2 sentences). To get this endeavor off the ground and cover some of the initial costs, I'll be launching a crowdfunding campaign to raise $_____. To reach this funding goal, I'm putting together a small team of advocates who can contribute approximately 10 hours during a month long campaign and help with the following:

- Social media, blogging
- Reaching out to potential influencers and contributors
- Planning a launch event
- (Include your own bullets here, the above are just a few common examples)

I'm reaching out to you because with your help in these areas, I'm confident that this campaign will be a success! Please let me know if you can help me realize this dream by joining my team. I'm currently working on my crowdfunding campaign strategy and would appreciate your advice. Is there a time when I can (meet/talk/skype) with you to go over what I've got so far?

Thank you for your time and help.

Sincerely,

(Your name)

5. When will you launch your crowdfunding campaign?

In general, statistics show that crowdfunding campaigns raise the most when they end sometime between April and September. On the other hand, the least amount of funding is raised in the fourth quarter[14].

 Crowdfunding Campaign Launch Date: _____

If you were able to answer yes to the previous four questions, then you should be able to pick the exact date you will launch your crowdfunding campaign, plus or minus a day.

6. Which holidays or observances happen during and after your crowdfunding campaign?

---

[14] Crowdsourcing.org. What is the Optimal Time of the Year to Launch your Kickstarter Campaign? 24 Sept. 2014. < http://www.crowdsourcing.org/editorial/what-is-the-optimal-time-of-the-year-to-launch-your-kickstarter-campaign/33861>

If your campaign coincides with a holiday or observance, you can craft your marketing message and include relevant perks/rewards for that occasion. For example, if your campaign will run from the mid-March to mid-April, you can include a Mother's Day (early May) themed perk/reward and marketing message. Just be sure that if you include a themed perk/reward and message that you can deliver and fulfill your obligations by that day. No one wants their Mother's Day themed perk/reward in June.

We've included a list of U.S holidays and popular observances in the appendix for your reference. List the holidays or observances that will occur during or after your crowdfunding campaign below:

_____

_____

_____

7. Which community events take place during your crowdfunding campaign?

Events that take place in your community during your campaign will offer an opportunity to meet new and like-minded people that could become your supporters and contributors. For example, speaking at a local chamber of commerce event about your project, joining a relevant meet-up group, going to a small business training, etc. are all ways to get attention to your campaign.

_____

_____

_____

_____

_____

8. Start to create your crowdfunding campaign calendar

Now that you know when you will start your campaign and how long it will last, you can begin to create your crowdfunding campaign calendar. The calendar allows you to schedule press releases, social media blasts, events and activities during your campaign. You can create a group calendar through Google so your entire team can add and update events and tasks.

Take into consideration some of the holidays, observances and community events that you identified above when making your schedule. How can you partake in or relate your activities to some of these events? As you continue with the checklist you'll be able to fill in a more detailed schedule.

Helpful Resource: Google's group calendars: https://support.google.com/a/answer/1626902?hl=en

9. Create an action plan.

If you've reached this point in the guide and still feel a bit unsure of where to start or what to do next, it's time to step back, create an action plan and accomplish one task at a time. I've created a Crowdfunding Campaign Action Plan and included it in the appendix. Use it to list the 3-5 most important things that need to be accomplished before anything else. If you're working within a team, you can identify who will be responsible for what. Set a deadline for each task and the resources required to accomplish it.

Helpful Resource: Crowdfunding Campaign Action Plan (located in the appendix)

Notes:

_____

_____

_____

_____

_____

_____

_____

_____

_____

_____

Establish and Enhance Your Online Presence

One of the first steps in beginning to execute your crowdfunding campaign is to establish, expand and enhance your online presence. Hopefully, you're able to say 'yes' to many of the questions below already. The more yeses, the higher your likelihood of having a wide enough network to support your campaign. If you're answering no to a lot of these questions, you've got a lot of prep work to do before you launch your campaign, but take advantage of the suggestions below to help guide you in the right direction.

1. **Do you have a website?**

   Approximately 70% of organizations believe that their website is an effective marketing activity[15]. If your crowdfunding campaign is the start of an ongoing project or the first step in launching your business or non-profit, then a website is something you'll want to have during and after the crowdfunding campaign.

Yes

Good deal! Make sure you've updated your website with current information. Ensure you have social media links on your website so contributors can follow you. Finally, link to your crowdfunding campaign from your home page.

No

If you don't have a website currently, it's a good idea to have one, even if it's just a simple landing page, before you launch and promote your campaign. A guide on how to build a website falls outside the scope of this publication, but here are some resources to help you get a website up and running:

- Get Your Business Online: www.gybo.com
  An initiative by Google and Intuit to help new and small businesses get a web presence free or at low cost.
- Fiverr®: www.fiverr.com
  Fiverr® is an amazing crowdsourcing platform that can connect you with freelancers from around the world willing to help you with a website starting at only $5!
- Elance®: https://www.elance.com
  Elance is another amazing crowdsourcing platform that can connect you with freelance designers and software developers from around the world.

A special note for non-profits:

Online donations to non-profits are becoming more popular. In fact, a recent survey by Blackbaud Target Analytics found that 39% of donors donated online between 2011 and 2013. Non-profits should leverage their websites and existing crowdfunding platforms to take advantage of this trend. The chart below shows how online donations compare to other fundraising channels.

---

[15] "Marketing strategies found to be effective by small businesses in the U.S 2012". Statista. Pew Research Center. 2012. Accessed 21 November 2013. University of Texas Libraries.

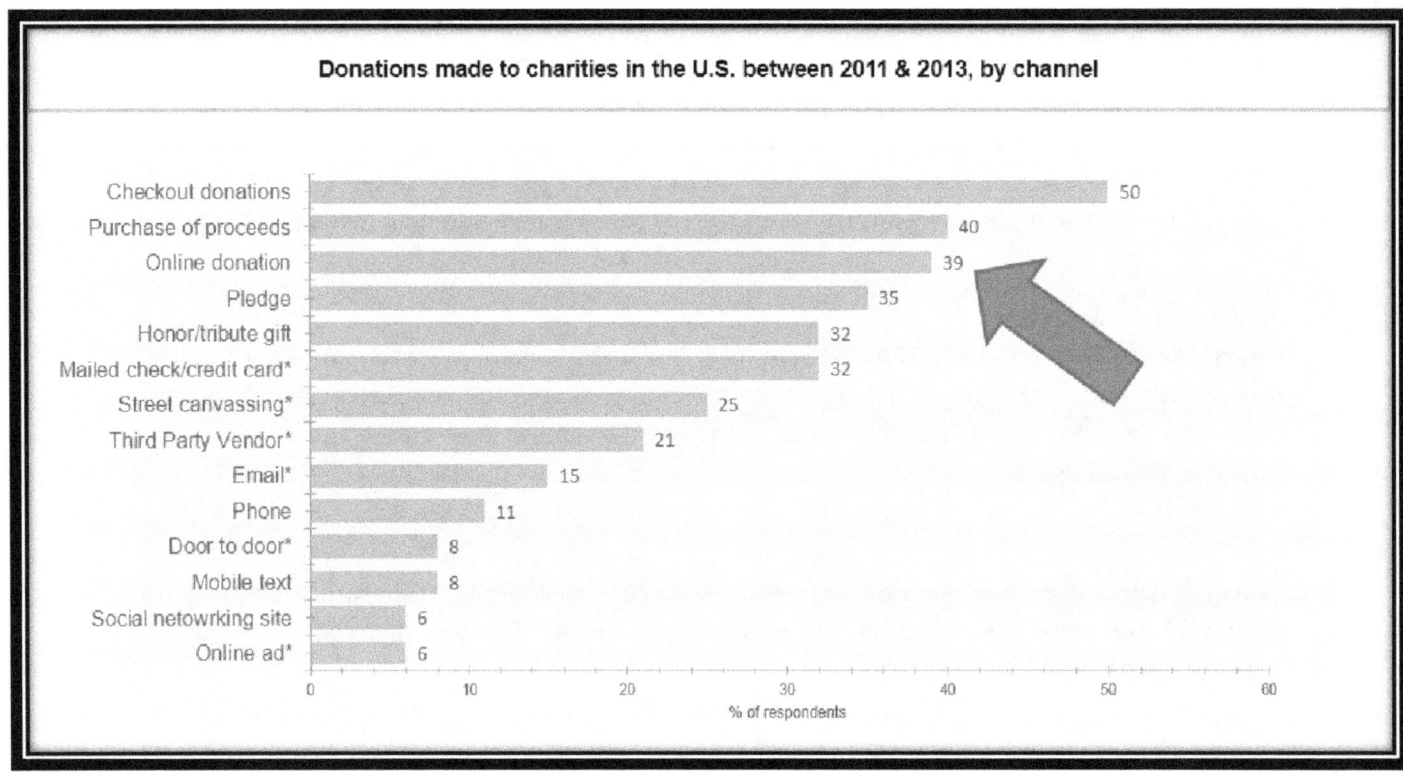

Figure 4: Donations made to charities in the U.S. between 2011 & 2013, by channel; Blackbaud, target analytics [16]

2. Are you on Facebook?

Yes

Like! Also, think about joining Facebook Groups that are relevant to your project. For example, I'm interested in helping start-up businesses in my hometown. A quick search of groups on Facebook shows a group called "Austin Startups". See what groups you can join and engage with.

No

At the time of this writing, Facebook is the largest social networking site in the world with approximately 1.27 billion users worldwide[17]. If you're not on Facebook, you need to get signed up and start expanding your friend network immediately.

---

[16] Blackbaud Target Analytics. Donations made to charity in the U.S. from 2011 to 2013, by channel used. Statista. Accessed 6 Feb 2014

[17] Facebook.com

Crowdfunders with 1000+ Facebook "friend" connections have up to a 40% higher chance of success[18]. It's free and easy to do! Facebook will play an important role during your crowdfunding campaign, so sign up now!

A special note for non-profits:

At the end of 2013, Facebook announced that it will start to offer a "Donate Now" button for non-profits[19]. At the time of this writing, this feature is still being piloted, but this may very well be Facebook's first strategic pivot into the crowdfunding space.

3. Are you on LinkedIn?

Approximately 1 out of 5 internet users in the U.S are on LinkedIn[20]. Are you one of those people?

Yes

Good! It's important to be on LinkedIn if you're planning to launch a crowdfunding campaign, especially because contributors can easily see how they're connected with you, who has endorsed you for skills or recommended you and what your past experiences have been. Make sure your LinkedIn profile is updated and you're gathering any relevant endorsements and recommendations you can. This will give you greater credibility.

No

 I highly recommend you join LinkedIn. It's free to join and it provides additional transparency and credibility for you and your project. You'll be able to connect with people you know, they'll be able to endorse you for certain skills or recommend you and you can share your relevant background and experiences with potential contributors.

In addition, once you've joined, you can search your network for people with certain skills you might need. For example, someone in your network might have PR experience and you can reach out to them to see if they can be an asset during your crowdfunding campaign.

4. Are you a member of any meet-up groups?

Meet-ups are grassroots associations organized through Meetup.com. Meet-ups are great because you can usually find a meet-up group relevant to your project. I'm also a big proponent of meet-ups because they combine online social media with in-person, face-to-face opportunities.

Yes

Sweet! Below, list the meet-up groups you belong to and indicate whether or not they're relevant to your project:

---

[18] Mollick, Ethan. The Dynamics of Crowdfunding: Determinants of Success and Failure. Jul 25. 2012. The Wharton School of the University of Pennsylvania.

[19] Facebook Launches Donate Button. http://www.huffingtonpost.com/2013/12/16/facebook-donate-button_n_4455275.html

[20] "Share of U.S. internet users who use LinkedIn in 2012". Statista. Pew Research Center. 2012. Accessed 21 November 2013. University of Texas Libraries.

Name of Meet-up group	Relevant to your project? (Yes or No)

Conduct a search on meetup.com for other relevant meet-ups that you can join. I've noticed a trend for crowdfunding meet-ups being organized. These meet-ups join you together with others interested in crowdfunding. Our organization created Keep Austin Funded as a meet-up group to bring entrepreneurs, non-profits, etc. together for networking, learning and resource sharing. If there isn't a crowdfunding meet-up group in your area, that may signal an opportunity for you to create one. Networking in a group like this can provide cross-promotional opportunities for your projects. Attend an upcoming meet-up and make connections that might benefit your project and crowdfunding campaign.

No

 Meetup.com offers a wide variety of different meet-up groups you can join. There's likely a meet-up group related to your project. For example, if your project is a non-profit initiative, there's likely several relevant meet-ups that involve non-profits. Also, many regions are forming crowdfunding meet-up groups. These groups provide excellent opportunities to network with other people contemplating or in the middle of their crowdfunding campaign. Most meet-ups are free and it's easy to join and quickly become an engaged member.

I recommend you sign up today and search for at least 3-4 relevant meet-ups in your area. List those meet-up groups below and indicate when their next meeting will be:

Name of relevant meetup.com group	Group's next scheduled meet-up	Meet-up organizer

5. Are you on Twitter?

In 2013 there were 31.8 million Twitter users in the United States alone and user growth is forecasted at more than 9% through 2014[21]. Research shows that, on average, successful crowdfunding campaigns tweeted 3.65 times more than unsuccessful campaigns, with an average of approximately 73 tweets throughout the duration of the campaign[22].

Yes

Tweet!

No

Because Twitter can provide access to a considerably sized audience, it's important to be actively engaged in their network. Like many of the other social media networks, Twitter is free and easy to sign up. You should be using Twitter to attract attention to your crowdfunding campaign.

6. Do you blog?

Yes

Write on! Your blog can help you enhance the presence of your project online. Make sure your blog is relevant to your project so you can bridge a coherent connection for your blog readers.

No

A self-published blog isn't an essential element in a successful crowdfunding campaign, but if you have ever considered blogging and feel you have something blog worthy to write about, it might be a good time to start as you plan your crowdfunding project. A blog is a great way to engage your most loyal stakeholders and attract a fresh audience with interesting content.

 I use Wordpress when I blog and find it extremely user friendly, while still providing options for customization. Some other popular blogging platforms include: Blogger and Tumblr.

7. Identify relevant bloggers or influencers in your community and/or industry?

An influencer is a network or individual with a high communication return on investment. This individual or group's endorsement or support can bring credibility and attention to your project. Influencers can be associations, other networks, community leaders and even bloggers with a large following. Nike, Hanes and Gatorade have all used Michael Jordan in their advertisements and marketing campaigns because he is a global influencer. You're probably not going to be able to get Jordan's endorsement for

---

[21] "Number of Adult U.S Twitter Users from 2010 to 2014". Statista. Source: Source: eMarketer. 2013. Accessed 22 November 2013. University of Texas Libraries.

[22] Etter, Vincent; Grossglauser, Matthias; Thiran, Patrick. "Launch Hard or Go Home – Predicting the Success of Kickstarter Campaigns". Oct. 2013. Accessed 22 November 2013 (http://www.crowdsourcing.org/editorial/researchers-can-predict-if-kickstarter-projects-will-succeed-within-4-hours/28919)

your project, but there are appropriate influencers and bloggers that can still have a measurable impact on your campaign. For example, if your project involves a new baby product, reach out to bloggers blogging about baby products. You might also look for influencers in your own community. For example, Austin's paper, the Austin American Statesman maintains the Homeroom Blog, a blog about education. If I were in Austin launching an education related campaign, I'd reach out to them to see if they'd be willing to write a story about me or my project.

When searching for bloggers or influencers, use keywords that are relevant to your project. You can also search on Fiverr® (fiverr.com) for gigs® from bloggers willing to write a blog about your project starting at a cost of only $5!

Search for at least 3-4 relevant bloggers or influencers in your community and/or industry and list them below:

Relevant blogger or key influencer	Email, website and other contact information

8. **Identify other relevant media outlets in your community and/or industry.**

Besides bloggers and key influencers, there may be opportunities to get exposure for your campaign in local and industry related media outlets. For example, the local chamber of commerce's publications, community newsletters, local newspaper, industry journals and newsletters, etc. Search for at least 3-4 relevant media outlets in your community or industry:

Relevant media outlet	Email, website and other contact information or notes on procedures for contacting

9. How far does your social network reach?

Now that you've enhanced your online presence, let's measure your online reach and set goals for continuing to expand your online networks. Answer the questions in the REV Assessment located in the appendix. Once you've filled in the answers for your current network reach, include goals for extending that reach.

Helpful Resource: Social Network REV Assessment

Notes:

_____

_____

_____

_____

_____

_____

_____

_____

Develop Desirable Perks and Rewards

Unless you're asking exclusively for donations, you'll want to have some exciting perks and rewards to offer your project backers. I've included a list of 50+ perks and rewards from successful campaigns in various industries in the appendix to help you brainstorm. Also, as you walk through this checklist, use the perks/rewards worksheet located in the appendix to jot down your ideas.

1. Are you offering your product or service as a perk/reward?

Yes

Superb. If possible, include various tiers or levels that your product or service can be priced at. For example, if you offer tutoring services, you can offer 1 hour for $20 or 2 hours for $35, etc. If you're offering a tangible product, like food, you can offer various serving size options at different prices.

No

Unless it's completely impossible or inapplicable, you always want to include your product or service as an available perk or reward. After all, your product or service is core to your project and the success you're trying to create. Even if you are a non-profit, you can ask donors to sponsor the individuals or groups that benefit from your service.

2. Have you considered conducting market research with your perks/rewards?

Crowdfunding provides a unique opportunity to conduct market research with early adopters. Early adopters are those consumers that are willing and likely to try your product or service before the broader market. Early adopters are those people you see standing in line waiting for the newest iPhone or video game. Use crowdfunding as an opportunity to learn from these early adopters.

For example, if you are offering massage services, you can offer one option for a massage in a person's home and another option for a massage at your regular place of business. Offering these two tiers of service at different price levels provides useful information that can be used beyond the crowdfunding campaign: is there demand for in-home massage services? How much are people willing to pay for in-home services?

You can also conduct market research with products. For example, let's say you're starting a line of footwear. You can offer different styles and colors to see which are most popular. Take this information and use it to forecast demand for your inventory beyond the crowdfunding campaign. Let the crowd provide important feedback about your offerings.

3. Are you offering "swag" as a perk/reward?

Swag refers to the promotional items like t-shirts, coffee mugs, key chains, USB thumb drives, sunglasses, bumper stickers, magnets, etc. that you often see offered as a perk/reward in crowdfunding campaigns.

Yes

Okay, but make sure you're offering something unique and complementary, if possible. For example, let's say you're crowdfunding a project related to education. Your first thought might be to offer a bumper sticker or t-shirt, but wouldn't a pencil, notebook or backpack make more sense? These items might also be more useful after the crowdfunding campaign. You can get some different ideas for the type of swag being offered by successful campaigns with the list of perks and rewards located in the appendix.

Also, take into consideration that swag costs money and so does shipping it to your backers. For whatever swag item you decide to offer as a perk or reward, you need to calculate the cost of the swag + shipping. You might be required to purchase your swag in bulk. For example, you probably won't be able to buy only 5 custom bumper stickers. I've seen plenty of crowdfunders with boxes of swag leftover from their campaigns because they had to buy in bulk to get the costs down. Use the perks and rewards worksheet located in the appendix to walk you through how to calculate your perk/reward costs.

No

Offering swag as a perk/reward isn't necessary, but it is quite common in crowdfunding campaigns. If you've got other exciting perks/rewards to offer and don't need to offer swag you might be better off, overall. However, one benefit of swag is that it can become useful marketing or promotional material after the crowdfunding campaign.

For example, if you'll be crowdfunding a project in the education industry, it might make sense to put your brand and logo on learning materials (pens, pencils, notebooks, etc). These materials will likely be useful after the campaign.

Helpful Resource: Perks and Rewards Worksheet

4. Have you partnered with a non-profit, church or other community organization to offer a perk/reward that also gives back?

One useful strategy, that I believe is underutilized, is partnering with a non-profit, community organization or religious institution to offer a socially conscious perk or reward outside of your core product and service offerings. For example, you could donate 10% of contributions for a specific perk/reward to support a local non-profit, church, etc.

Obviously, you'll want to reach out to the non-profit, church or community organization and get their permission beforehand, but this is a really great way to extend your network while simultaneously giving back to the community. Make sure you ask the organization if they will leverage their social media, newsletters, meetings, etc to give exposure to your project and/or the perk/reward designed to benefit them. Embrace the mindset that we can all accomplish more by working together.

Yes

Good! By giving, you'll receive more.

No

If you're a non-profit or social enterprise, this question might not be applicable to you. Also, if you're planning to crowdfund on Kickstarter, they will not allow this type of perk/reward. Otherwise, I would strongly consider the mutual benefits of partnering with these types of organizations.

5. **Have you searched for successful campaigns related to your project to see what they've offered as a perk/reward?**

Yes

Good, use the perks and rewards worksheet in the appendix to jot down some of the best ideas you come across.

No

I've included a short list of 50 perk/reward ideas from successful campaigns in the appendix, but it's a good idea to search for other successful case studies related to your project. Try searching Kickstarter and Indiegogo with keywords related to your project and find successful campaigns that you can pull perk/reward ideas from.

Helpful Resource: Perks and Rewards Worksheet

Helpful Resource: Perks and Rewards Idea List

6. **Have you created perks/rewards that align with popular holidays or observances that occur during your campaign?**

When you planned your crowdfunding timeline, you identified holidays and observances that will occur during your campaign. Is it appropriate to create a perk/reward that integrates the theme of the holiday or occasion? For example, if the 4th of July occurs during your crowdfunding campaign, you can offer a perk/reward around an Independence Day theme: red, white and blue, U.S flag, Uncle Sam, fireworks, etc.

Yes

Great. If you've created a reward for a specific holiday or observance, make sure that you can fulfill that reward on or before the holiday. For example, you don't want to market a perk/reward as a great Christmas gift, but deliver it at the end of January.

No

It may not be appropriate to create perks/rewards around a holiday theme. For example, if I were to crowdfund this book during Valentine's Day, I'm not sure I could pitch it as a gift for your sweetie. However, if I ran the campaign during Small Business Week in November, I'd most definitely frame my marketing message and perks/rewards to ride the coat tails of the already established media for that observance.

7. Have you created a reward that will be introduced after the campaign has started?

Campaigns that introduce a new reward after their campaign has started have a greater chance of success[23]. As you plan what perks/rewards you'll offer, create one or two that you'll keep in your back pocket and introduce after the campaign has started. This helps keep your campaign fresh and exciting. The Perks/Rewards Worksheet includes a section for this special perk/reward.

Yes

Excellent! Make sure you also send out a special notice to update backers and potential contributors about the new offering.

No

It's a good idea to plan for a perk/reward that you'll introduce after the campaign has launched. Even if you never use this perk/reward, it's a good idea to brainstorm about it now and include it in your Perks and Rewards Worksheet.

Helpful Resource: Perks and Rewards Worksheet

8. Have you created perks/rewards that you can fulfill within a reasonable timeframe?

A reasonable timeframe will largely depend on your project. The important thing is to set realistic expectations for the crowd about when they can reasonably expect to receive their perk/reward. It's better to under-promise and over-deliver. If you think you can deliver your product 6 weeks after the campaign, tell the crowd to expect it in 8-10 weeks. As with any project, there are usually unforeseen delays. If you deliver early, your backers will be delighted. If you deliver late, you'll be bombarded with emails and unhappy backers.

Yes

Good, now add about 30% to that estimate and that's the timeline you can tell the crowd to expect. Remember, always under-promise and over-deliver, whenever possible.

No

That's okay, but make sure you set a realistic expectation for backers. If your project is a manned mission to Mars and you've promised backers a rock from the Red Planet, it's likely that this reward will take years to fulfill. If you're clear and up-front, the crowd will have to accept the fulfillment timeline

---

[23] Xu, Anbang; Yang, Xiao; Rao, Huaming; Fu, Wai-Tat; Huang, Shih-Wen; Bailey, Brian. "Show me the Money! An Analysis of Project Updates during Crowdfunding Campaigns". 2014

you've set. This doesn't mean that you won't still receive emails from impatient backers, but you can simply remind them of the timeline you outlined instead of having to explain delays.

9. **Offer perks/rewards at appropriate tiers and intervals.**
   Make sure you're offering your perks/rewards at appropriate tiers and intervals. Use the levels below and perk/reward examples in the appendix as a guide:

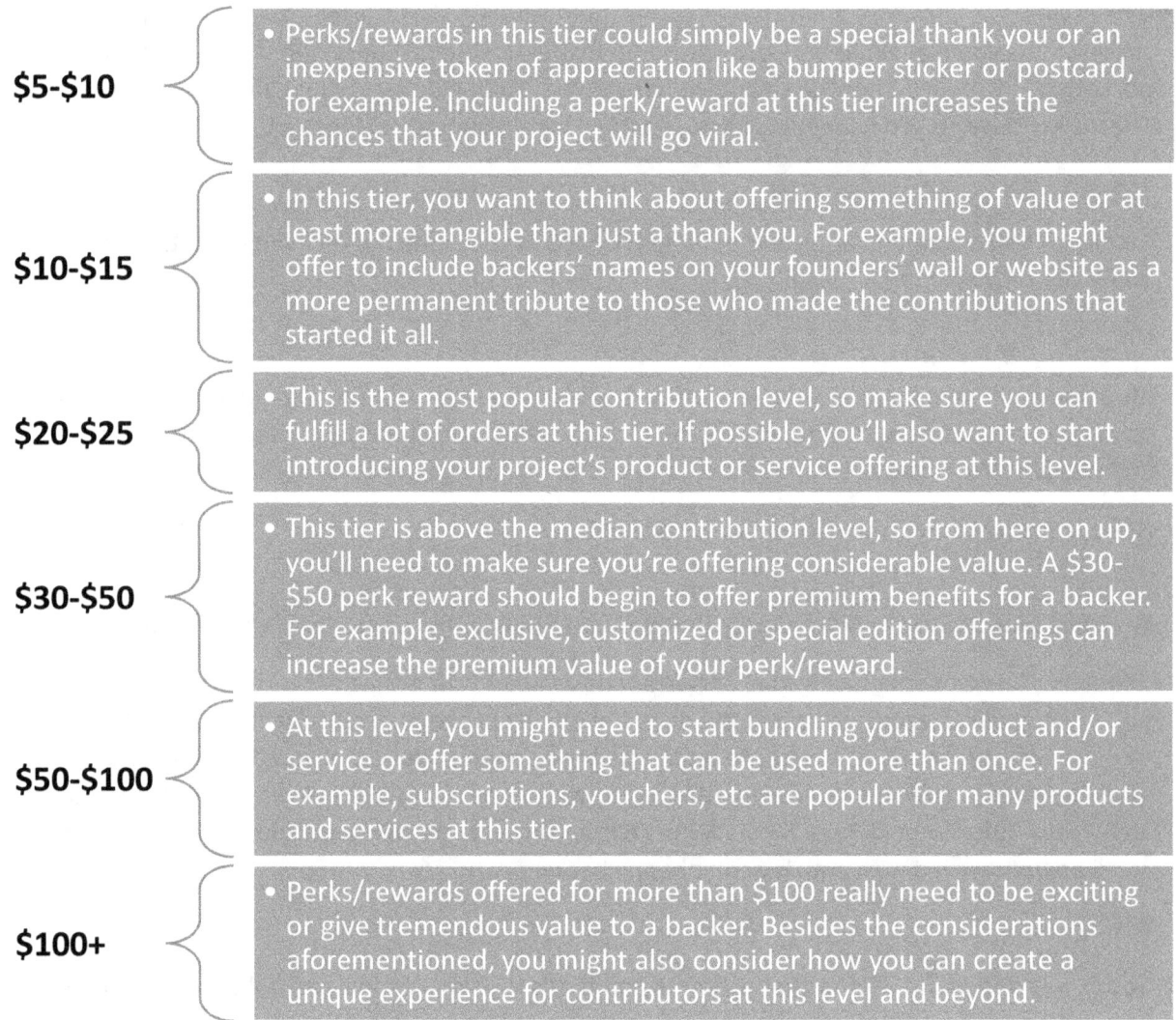

$5-$10
- Perks/rewards in this tier could simply be a special thank you or an inexpensive token of appreciation like a bumper sticker or postcard, for example. Including a perk/reward at this tier increases the chances that your project will go viral.

$10-$15
- In this tier, you want to think about offering something of value or at least more tangible than just a thank you. For example, you might offer to include backers' names on your founders' wall or website as a more permanent tribute to those who made the contributions that started it all.

$20-$25
- This is the most popular contribution level, so make sure you can fulfill a lot of orders at this tier. If possible, you'll also want to start introducing your project's product or service offering at this level.

$30-$50
- This tier is above the median contribution level, so from here on up, you'll need to make sure you're offering considerable value. A $30-$50 perk reward should begin to offer premium benefits for a backer. For example, exclusive, customized or special edition offerings can increase the premium value of your perk/reward.

$50-$100
- At this level, you might need to start bundling your product and/or service or offer something that can be used more than once. For example, subscriptions, vouchers, etc are popular for many products and services at this tier.

$100+
- Perks/rewards offered for more than $100 really need to be exciting or give tremendous value to a backer. Besides the considerations aforementioned, you might also consider how you can create a unique experience for contributors at this level and beyond.

10. **Create a description of your perks/rewards to include in your campaign description.**

Now that you have your perks and rewards identified, it's time to create a description of them for backers. You'll want to provide a general description of the perk/reward. If you're offering swag, include a picture of what a contributor will be receiving.

The Fiverr.com Perks/Rewards Strategy

I'm a huge fan of Fiverr.com®, the crowdsourcing website where talented people from around the world offer their skills and services starting at just $5.00 USD. I worked with a consortium of nonprofits to come up with some perks and rewards for their crowdfunding project, The Community Loan Center (CLC). The CLC sought to raise funds to create a loan pool to use as an alternative to predatory and usurious pay day loan and auto title loans. This consortium of nonprofits didn't have much to offer as a tangible perk/reward, so we sourced Fiverr® for some creative ideas. Since the service offered is lending, we tried to tie our perks and rewards around the theme of money, but at the same time make the rewards fun and unique. Here's what we came up with:

The Handwritten Thank You

A beautifully handwritten thank you letter mailed anywhere in the U.S (extra postage for international). The great thing about this Fiverr® Gig™ is that the letter writer takes care of all the mailing too.

Total Cost (Including Shipping): $6.25 each for 1 letter; $4.25 each for 5 or more letters.
Level of contribution: $25.00+
Surplus per unit: $21.75

The Superhero Thank You

A superhero caricature illustrated in the contributor's image. This is a neat way to say thank you in a personalized and unique way.

Total Cost: $5.00
Level of contribution: $35.00
Surplus per unit: $30.00

A Penny for your Thoughts

Since the project is related to lending and saving, we tried to create perks/rewards that were relevant to that theme. One Fiverr® Gig™ offered a personalized U.S penny keychain or necklace. You can choose what you want to have engraved on the penny. For example, a contributor's initials or a simple 'thank you'.

Total Cost (Including Shipping): $9.00
Level of contribution: $45.00
Surplus per unit: $36.00

Bronze, Silver, Gold Level Sponsors

Donors receive recognition with their name or business engraved into a digital bronze coin that will be proudly displayed on the organization's About Us page. It costs nothing to just incorporate text, but if you wanted an image engraved, there are a few artists on Fiverr who offer that service.

Total Cost: $0.00 for just text (do it yourself); $5.00 for engraving
Level of contribution: Bronze $50.00; Silver $100; Gold $250
Surplus per unit: $45.00+

A Comic Wallet

There's nothing comical about predatory lending, but helping people save money can be fun. Store those savings in a wallet made from comic books and laminated for durability.

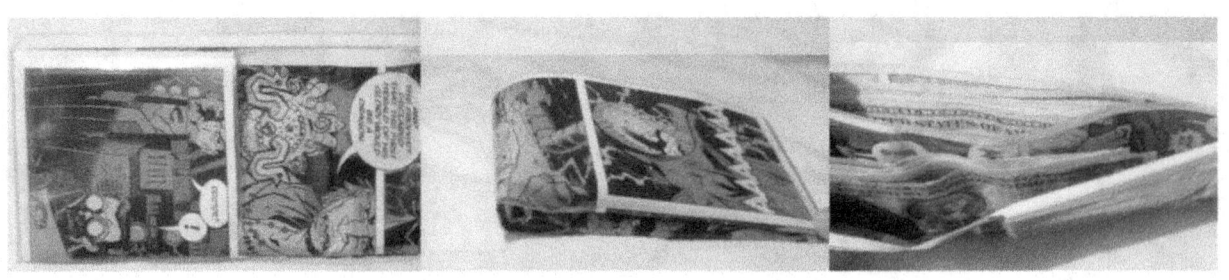

Total Cost (Including Shipping): $15.00
Level of contribution: $75.00
Surplus per unit: $60.00

Special note for those interested in crowdfunding on Kickstarter.com

The following items are things that cannot be offered as a perk or reward on Kickstarter.com[24]:

- Any item claiming to cure, treat, or prevent an illness or condition
- Contests, coupons, gambling, raffles, and lifetime memberships.
- Energy food and drinks.
- Offensive material (e.g., hate speech, encouraging violence against others, etc).
- Offering a genetically modified organism as a reward.
- Offering alcohol as a reward.
- Offering financial, money-processing, or credit services; financial intermediaries or cash-equivalent instruments; travel services (e.g., vacation packages); phone services (e.g., prepaid phone services, 900 numbers); and business marketing services.
- Political fundraising.
- Pornographic material.
- Resale. All rewards must have been produced or designed by the project or one of its creators — no reselling things from elsewhere.
- Tobacco, drugs, and drug paraphernalia.
- Weapons, replicas of weapons, and weapon accessories.

Notes:

_____

_____

_____

_____

---

[24] https://www.kickstarter.com/rules/prohibited

Produce an Effective Video Pitch

Having a video is absolutely critical to conveying an effective message and story about why your project is worthy of the crowd's funds. In fact, you're approximately 20%+ more likely to have a successful crowdfunding campaign if you have a video[25]. Do not post or promote your crowdfunding campaign without a video!

Produce an Effective Video Pitch

Having a video is absolutely critical to conveying an effective message and story about why your project is worthy of the crowd's funds. In fact, you're 20% more like to have a successful crowdfunding campaign if you have a video. The questions below will make sure you're on track to making a great video.

Can you produce the video yourself?

Although it's not absolutely necessary to have a professional looking video in order to be successful, it is absolutely essential to have a video that compels a person to contribute funds to a campaign. If you can't produce the video yourself, find someone in your first level network who can help or budget for video services.

Have you created a storyboard?

Preparing a storyboard will save you time and help the storyline flow smoothly. Use our example and template in the appendix to help you create your storyboard.

Does it tell a great story?

Yours should convey the four P's of a great story:
~Purpose: What's the mission?
~Peril: Convey the challenge and frame it with a sense of urgency.
~Personality: Connect with people on a personal level.
~Proposition: Close the story with a call to action. Make the ask through an appeal or invitation.

Do you personally appear in the video?

If you do, the audience is more likely to connect with the project. Your appearance offers transparency and helps build trust with contributors.

Is your video less than 3 minutes?

You're more likely to retain the audience's attention with a video lasting 3 minutes or less. If your video is longer, you run the risk of losing the audience's attention. We recommend that you use the storyboard template located in the appendix to ensure that your video is concise and incoporates all the key segments.

Have you uploaded your video online?

Most crowdfunding platforms don't allow you to upload your video directly to their site. Instead, they'll ask that you link to YouTube or Vimeo, two of the most popular video hosting sites.

---

[25] Mollick, Ethan. The Dynamics of Crowdfunding: Determinants of Success and Failure. Jul 25. 2012. The Wharton School of the University of Pennsylvania.

1. Who is your target audience? _____

It's important that you identify a target audience for your product or service. Many people will mistakenly claim that everyone is part of their target market, but that's rarely the case. Everyone may be a potential customer, but your efforts and resources should be directed toward a target audience that is most likely to buy.

The same logic is applicable to crowdfunding and your video message should be aimed at the target market most likely to contribute. If your target market is comprised mainly of families, then you'll want to make sure you have images of happy families in your marketing materials. If you haven't identified your target market, you should stop here and reevaluate your market analysis and strategy before moving forward.

2. Do you have the willingness and capability to produce the video yourself?

Yes

Excellent! That's one less thing to worry about. Regardless of your skill level in videography, however, you might find it helpful to go through the rest of the checklist, even if it's just a quick refresher on some things.

Unsure

Although it's not absolutely necessary to have a professional looking video in order to be successful, it is absolutely essential to have a video that compels a person to contribute funds to a campaign. A video that is distracting because the camera is shaky or the sound of the wind distorting the audio, for example, could deter potential funders. If you don't have much experience filming and editing, then I suggest you look for a resource to help.

If you're going to give it a shot yourself, then you want to have a decent video capture device; most new camera phones will suffice. Also, you'll need access to some type of editing software. Most personal computers (PC or Mac) will come with entry level software that is sufficient.

I also highly recommend watching a couple of tutorial videos with Vimeo's Video School to help familiarize yourself with some video production basics.

No

If you're unable, unwilling or uncomfortable producing your crowdfunding video then you'll need to find a resource to help. Before spending money on video production services, think if there is anyone you know in your first level network who has the skills to produce an effective video.

    a. List anyone in your family or close circle of friends with video production skills:

       _____

       _____

If you were able to identify at least one person above, then reach out and ask if they'd be willing to produce your crowdfunding campaign video. Maybe they owe you a favor, don't mind doing you a favor or would be interested in bartering.

If you were not able to identify at least one person above, then you're going to have to budget for video production services. I recommend you seek a local resource and if possible a small business or freelance videographer. You might also think about trying to find a student studying radio, television, film, animation, etc. These types of videographers and aspiring videographers could potentially be building their portfolios and might be able to cut you a deal on their fees. If they're unable to reduce their rate, ask them if they'd be willing to be flexible on payment terms, taking half up front and half once you've successfully completed your campaign.

Check your local business listing and social media network to see if you can locate an affordable videographer. Once you've negotiated price, be sure to include the costs of service back into your total project cost.

Helpful Resource*:* Vimeo's Video School (https://vimeo.com/videoschool)

3. Have you created a storyboard for your video?

Yes

Great! Compare it with our storyboard example below and feel free to use our template in the appendix to make any modifications you feel are necessary before filming. Also, continue with the guidelines below to help you measure the impact of your video's content.

No

Preparing a storyboard before filming will save you time and help the narrative and storyline flow much more smoothly. Use our example below and template in the appendix to help you create your storyboard. Read through the entire section on how to produce an effective video before creating your storyboard.

Helpful Resource*:* Storyboard example (located below and in the appendix)

Helpful Resource*:* Storyboard template (located in the appendix)

Smart tip: Avoid jargon, keep it simple.

Keep your message simple and free of tech speak or jargon. You should assume that the majority of your audience will have never heard of the technical terms that describe your project.

You can always outline the technical specifications in supporting documentation so that people who are adept on the subject have a place to find their answers as well.

Introduction narrative

Introduce yourself and the project. The introduction should be no longer than 15-20 seconds.

"Hello, my name is Lance McNeill. As a small business coach and adviser, I'm especially excited about the possibilities and opportunities that crowdfunding can offer existing businesses and aspiring entrepreneurs! Through my customers' extensive research and experience, I've developed the first comprehensive guide for perks/rewards based crowdfunding."

How much time did it take you to clearly narrate the introduction (In seconds)?

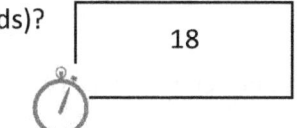

18

Introduction visuals

Describe the visual scene or animation happening alongside the narrative. Include an estimate of how long each scene will appear and make sure that, summed together, the scenes equal the time it takes to narrate the introduction.

Visual scene or animation	Length of scene (In seconds)
Filming me as I introduce myself. I'll be in or around some recognizable small businesses.	11-12
Filming the cover of the guide or me holding the guide while speaking	6-7

Narrate the need or market pain that your project will address. Hit the high points and keep it brief. Statistics are great to include in this section. The description of the need shouldn't be longer than 20 seconds.

"You've probably heard some of the amazing success stories made possible with the help of crowdfunding platforms like Kickstarter or Indiegogo, but did you know that more than half of projects on those platforms are unsuccessful because they never reach their fundraising goal? There's a lot that goes into the planning and execution of a successful crowdfunding campaign, but platforms aren't offering a much needed comprehensive, step-by-step guide."

How much time did it take you to clearly narrate the need or market pain (In seconds)?

19-20

Need or market pain visuals

Describe the visual scene or animation happening alongside the narrative. Include an estimate of how long each scene will appear and make sure that, summed together, the scenes equal the time it takes to narrate the introduction.

Visual scene or animation	Length of scene (In seconds)
Screenshot of some of the successful campaigns on Kickstarter and/or Indiegogo	5-6
Infographic/slide of crowdfunding portal/platform success rates: Kickstarter = approximately 44%; Indiegogo = approximately 36%	6-7
Animation of words that represent all the many considerations that should go into a successful crowdfunding campaign falling or moving in a chaotic or disorganized manner.	4-5
Animation of those same words being aligned and organized in an orderly fashion like a list, for example.	4-5

Project description and solution narrative

Effectively convey what your project is and why or how it addresses the need, market pain or challenge you described in the previous narrative. Don't just describe your project, tell the audience why it is a compelling solution. In the first section of this guide, we had you identify your project's unique value propositions. Make sure you're including those propositions or differentiators in this narrative. The length of this section will vary depending on the complexity of the project and solution offered. However, as a general guideline, this narrative will be 30-120 seconds long.

"That's why I've created the first ever comprehensive guide for perks & rewards based crowdfunding! This detailed, step-by-step guide will show you how to plan, launch and execute a successful crowdfunding campaign. With our thorough checklist and easy to follow question/answer guide, you'll not only have access to best practices and helpful tools, but you'll also have a better understanding of when and how to use them.

Let our guide walk you through how to more accurately determine your project costs, realistically plan your campaign timeline, establish or enhance your on-line presence, create exciting perks and rewards and produce an effective video pitch and much, much more!"

Testimonial:

"I knew I wanted to raise money for my small business through crowdfunding, but I wasn't sure what my first step should be. The crowdfunding guide and checklist lead me step-by-step in the right direction and I successfully raised the money I needed to get my business off the ground!"

How much time did it take you to clearly narrate the project description and solution (In seconds)?

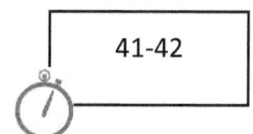

41-42

Project description and solution visuals

Describe the visual scene or animation happening alongside the narrative. Include an estimate of how long each scene will appear and make sure that, summed together, the scenes equal the time it takes to narrate the introduction.

Visual scene or animation	Length of scene (In seconds)
Visual of the crowdfunding guide, showing the checklist and steps in the guide	10-11
Testimonial using the guide and filling out the worksheets	9-10
Showing the testimonial's project costs worksheet, campaign calendar, snippet from testimonial's crowdfunding video.	10
Screenshots from testimonial's crowdfunding campaign	10-11

Conclusion and "ask" narrative

Now that you've made an introduction, described a need or market pain, described your project and offered a solution, it's time to ask the crowd to contribute. Make sure you tell them specifically what their contribution will help you fund. This narrative should last no longer than 20 seconds.

"I created this guide for you, with the entrepreneur and non-profit fundraiser in mind, because I want to see more people gain access to the capital they need to reach their goals. Crowdfunding is undeniably revolutionary in the way we access funds for our early stage projects, but it's still a very new frontier. Let this handbook be your guiding light. Make your contribution now and take advantage of the exciting perks and rewards we have to offer and get your own copy of the guide plus much more."

How much time did it take you to clearly narrate the conclusion and make the "ask"? (In seconds)

23-24

Conclusion and ask visuals

Describe the visual scene or animation happening alongside the narrative. Include an estimate of how long each scene will appear and make sure that, summed together, the scenes equal the time it takes to narrate the introduction.

Visual scene or animation	Length of scene (In seconds)
Filming in front of local businesses and/or non-profits	17-18
Screenshot or slides of perks/rewards being offered	6-7

4. Does your storyboard tell a great story?

Yes

Right on! Your video conveys the four P's of a great story: purpose, peril, personality and proposition. If you're not quite confident that you've addressed the four P's, check below.

Unsure

Your project should include the four P's of a great story:

- **Purpose** – what's the mission, vision and unique value proposition?
- **Peril** – Convey the need, challenge or market pain and frame it with a sense of urgency or around a limited window of opportunity
- **Personality** – Connect with people on a personal level and tell the story of self.
- **Proposition** – Close the story with a call to action. Clearly explain what is needed and make "the ask" through a provocative appeal or welcome invitation.

No

Use the four P's of a great story and the storyboard template to help you craft a compelling story for your video!

Southside Chicago's Celebration Playground

Project: Community Playground
Amount raised: $44,799
Campaign duration: 60 days
Crowdfunding platform: Indiegogo

Ann Luban's son, Mark, and Maxine Handelman's daughter, Ariana, are best friends. When Ariana and Mark came to their parents with the idea to help build a playground in the historically underserved Bronzeville neighborhood in the Southside of Chicago, Ann and Maxine were inspired to help. Since they had no idea how to start building a playground, they reached out to Kaboom! Kaboom is a nonprofit that helps organizations build playgrounds. Kaboom offered the logistical and project management support, but Ann and Maxine needed funding to make it all happen.

First, they turned to corporate sponsors, but didn't receive the enthusiastic response they were hoping for, so they decided to create a grassroots fundraising effort through crowdfunding. Their message included the four P's that make a great story:

Purpose: Build a playground

Peril: Without funding, there would be no playground.
Personality: Their video was compelling, in my opinion, because they highlighted their target beneficiaries – kids. It gave the project personality and who can resist cute kids asking for help to build a playground?
Proposition: At the end of the video, 20 kids chanted in unison, "Help build the playground"!

The video starts with kids playing on a playground, smiling and having fun. Ann and Maxine were given permission to use some of Kaboom's previous footage to show the building of a playground. This helped show that the project had a tangible outcome – a playground. The idea for the playground was originated by their kids, so they appropriately showcased testimonials from kids in the crowdfunding video. Whenever possible, promote your project or program beneficiaries in the crowdfunding video.

The two video strategy

Ann and Maxine did something else that was unique and effective, they created a second video, which they released after the campaign had already started. The video featured their kids singing an adorable song they wrote about building a playground. The video was simple and fun and reenergized the campaign when they released it with approximately 13 days of fundraising left. This was important because the Celebration Playground project surpassed its fundraising goal of $30,000 with a considerable amount of time to spare. The second video helped keep the excitement and momentum of the campaign going, giving attention to the project's stretch goals and encouraging additional donations.

5. Do you and/or your project's beneficiaries personally appear in the video?

Yes

Alright! When you personally appear in the video, the audience is more likely to connect with the project. Your appearance offers transparency and helps build trust with contributors. Make sure you've introduced yourself and explained why you have credibility when it comes to this specific project. Also, as was just highlighted in the Chicago Celebration Playground case study, putting beneficiaries at the forefront of the video can be very effective.

No

As the project creator, it's important to be as transparent as possible in order to build trust with contributors. You should appear in the video within the first 20 seconds. We highly recommend you begin your video by introducing yourself and sharing the specific experience, education, background, knowledge, skills or abilities that make you a credible project leader. Use the storyboard example and template to help guide you.

6. Is your video less than 3 minutes long?

Yes

Well done! You're more likely to retain the audience's attention with a video lasting 3 minutes or less. In fact, for most projects a video lasting between 1-2 minutes is ideal, but some projects, especially more technical or complex projects, might require a little more time.

No

If your video is longer than 3 minutes, you run a higher risk of losing the audience's attention before you're able to effectively convey your message and make an emotional appeal. I recommend that you use the storyboard template located in the appendix to ensure that your video is concise and incorporates all the key segments.

7. Have you uploaded your video to YouTube or Vimeo?

Most crowdfunding platforms don't allow you to upload your video directly to their site. Instead, they'll ask that you link to YouTube or Vimeo, two of the most popular video hosting sites.

If you need help creating an account on YouTube or Vimeo, visit their websites for step-by-step guides and tutorials to get you started.

Yes

Excellent. Make sure the thumbnail image for your video shows a relevant and appropriate screenshot. You've probably seen video thumbnails that are awkward still images of someone's mouth half opened mid-sentence. The best thumbnail is an image that provides useful or relevant information about your project. For example, your logo or a picture of your product make for great thumbnails.

You can create custom thumbnail images for your video on YouTube if your account is "verified and in good standing," otherwise you will be provided with three thumbnail options randomly generated[26]. Check out YouTube's step-by-step instructions for creating a custom thumbnail image for your video using the link below under helpful resources.

Choosing an appropriate thumbnail on Vimeo is much easier. Vimeo gives you several random images from your video to choose from and there aren't any account restrictions for choosing your own image.

No

Make sure you do several days before launching your campaign. You don't want to run into any technical difficulties with uploading your video the same day you plan to launch. Also, read the suggestions above about creating an appropriate thumbnail image for your video.

Helpful Resources:

 YouTube's instructions for creating custom thumbnail images for your video
https://support.google.com/youtube/answer/72431?hl=en

 Vimeo's instructions for creating custom thumbnail images for your video:
http://vimeo.com/help/faq/managing-your-videos/video-settings#how-do-i-change-the-thumbnail-of-my-video

---

[26] https://support.google.com/youtube/answer/72431?hl=en

8. Create an action plan.

If you've reached this point in the guide and still feel a bit unsure of where to start or what to do next, it's time to step back, create an action plan and accomplish one task at a time. I've created a Crowdfunding Campaign Action Plan and included it in the appendix. Use it to list the 3-5 most important things that need to be accomplished before anything else. If you're working within a team, you can identify who will be responsible for what. Set a deadline for each task and the resources required to accomplish it.

Online video is growing at a rapid pace. In fact, online video viewing is growing at an average of 16% per year among those aged 18-34[27]. Video has become an integral part of online advertising, but how can one create an effective video for fundraising. The two case studies below offer some practical tips.

When it comes to creating a viral video, it's 99.9% luck and the rest is in the art and intention. In 2012, the Invisible Children's Kony 2012 video became the most viral video ever to blaze across the internet with more than 100 million views in just six days[28]! Invisible Children, based in California, intended to bring attention to child soldiers in the Lord's Resistance Army (LRA) led by Joseph Kony in Uganda. Jason Russell, a documentary film maker and co-founder of Invisible Children, created the viral video using three key components:

1. **Personal and relatable**
   - Russell told the story from his own point of view and conveyed how it personally affected him and his family. He even recruited his own son to appear in the video.

2. **Simple**
   - The story of child soldiers is complex, but the video simplified the issue for the audience.

3. **A meaningful call to action**
   - The emotional appeal was designed to create passion in the audience, but the video created an outlet for that passion by detailing exactly how someone could take meaningful action.

The 2014 amyotrophic lateral sclerosis (ALS) Association's ice bucket challenge offers another interesting example of how a grassroots viral video can be used in fundraising. The ice bucket challenge kicked off in the summer of 2014 and between July 29th and August 29th, the ALS Association had raised $100.9 million in donations – a 3,500% increase in the amount of donations from the same period the year before[29]. The ice bucket challenge had two very unique things that helped it catch on:

1. **Sense of urgency**
   - At the end of each ice bucket challenge, the drenched and shivering participant challenged a few people to also partake in the ice bucket challenge and/or make a donation – either of which had to be completed in 24 hours.
2. **Direct appeal**
   - Not only did participants create a sense of urgency by giving those that they challenged 24 hours to respond, but they also called them out by name. This helped the challenge spread like wildfire on Facebook.

---

[27] Shifts in Viewing: The Cross Platform Report Q2 2014. Nielsen
http://www.nielsen.com/us/en/insights/reports/2014/shifts-in-viewing-the-cross-platform-report-q2-2014.html
[28] "Viral Video Power." CIO Magazine. (May 16, 2012): 1175 words. LexisNexis Academic. Web. Date Accessed: 2014/07/15.
[29] Landen, Rachel. "Ice Bucket Challenge offer invigorating fundraising lessons". Modern Healthcare. 1 Sept. 2014.

Notes:

_____

_____

_____

_____

_____

_____

_____

Choose the Right Crowdfunding Platform

Choosing the appropriate crowdfunding platform for your donation or perks/rewards based project is important. People will often use Kickstarter as a synonym for crowdfunding, but there are many more options besides just Kickstarter. Kickstarter is by far the most popular platform, but you might be surprised to learn that more than half of all projects on Kickstarter fail to reach their fundraising goal:

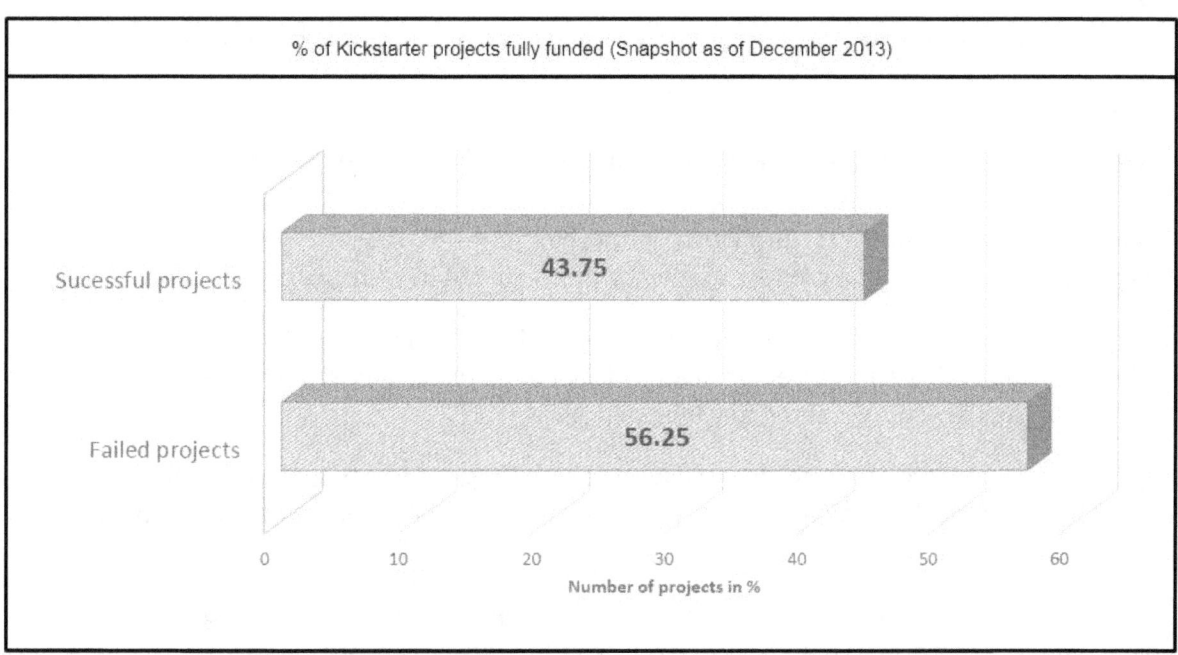

% of Kickstarter projects fully funded (Snapshot as of December 2013)

Figure 5: % of Kickstarter Project Fully Funded, Source: kickstarter.com/help/stats

If you're only familiar with a few platform options or you're not sure which platform to choose, use the information below to help guide you.

1. With which of the following categories does your project most closely relate?

☐ **Creative arts**
Examples: music, film, performing arts, photography
Creative arts projects comprised approximately 20% of all crowdfunding campaigns in 2012[30].

☐ **Personal causes**
Examples: A personal tragedy that you or a close loved one has experienced or is currently experiencing, personal development goal like obtaining funding to further education, etc.

☐ **Entrepreneurial/Small business**
Examples: food trailer, coffee shop, retail, services, software as a service, etc.

---

[30] Crowdsourcing.org, Crowdfunding.nl, Fundable. Statista 2014.
<http://www.statista.com.ezproxy.lib.utexas.edu/statistics/269975/most-active-crowdfunding-categories-of-2012/>

☐ **Invention/Innovation**
Examples: new consumer product idea, improvement of an existing product, etc.

☐ **Medical**
Examples: medical IT, health services, therapeutic products**, etc.**

☐ **Non-profit**
Examples: 501©3 non-profit yearly fundraiser, seed funding for new non-profit, etc.

☐ **Public Projects**
Examples: new public bike rack, park improvements, additional crosswalks, etc.

☐ **Social entrepreneurship or for-profit/non-profit hybrid**
Examples: non-profit with a product to sell, for-profit guided by a strong social mission.

It isn't necessary to crowdfund on a specialized platform. For example, Foodstart and Medstartr are specialized platforms that are focused on one particular industry as opposed to IndieGoGo or RocketHub, which allow for just about any type of project.

However, most specialized platforms have custom services and resources specific to your industry. Medstartr, for example, has a mentoring service that connects aspiring entrepreneurs in the medical field with industry experts[31].

Based on the categories above, here are some crowdfunding platforms you might consider. A more complete directory of platforms can be found online at Crowdsourcing.org:
http://www.crowdsourcing.org/directory

Creative arts
IndieGoGo (www.indiegogo.com)
Kickstarter (www.kickstarter.com)
RocketHub (www.rockethub.com)

Personal causes
Fundrazr (www.fundrazr.com)
GiveForward (www.giveforward.com)
GoFundMe (www.gofundme.com)
Indiegogo (www.indiegogo.com)
Tilt (www.tilt.com)

Entrepreneurial/Small business
Fundable (www.fundable.com)
Indiegogo (www.indiegogo.com)

Food
Foodstart (www.foodstart.com)
IndieGoGo (www.indiegogo.com)

Invention/Innovation
Kickstarter (www.kickstarter.com)
Vovation (www.vovation.com)

Medical
Medstartr (www.medstartr.com)

Non-profit
Community Funded
(http://communityfunded.com/)
Crowdrise (www.crowdrise.com)
Crowdtilt (www.crowdtilt.com)
Indiegogo (www.indiegogo.com)
StartSomeGood (www.startsomegood.com)

---

[31] http://about.medstartr.com/mentors/

Public Projects (civic crowdfunding)
Citizinvestor (www.citizinvestor.com)
Neighbor.ly (www.neighbor.ly)

Real Estate
Fundrise (www.fundrise.com)

Social Entrepreneurship/non-profit, for-profit hybrid
Crowdtilt (www.crowdtilt.com)
RocketHub (www.rockethub.com)
StartSomeGood (www.startsomegood.com)
WhenYouWish (www.whenyouwish.com)

2. **How much will you owe in crowdfunding fees?**

   Most crowdfunding platforms take a success fee, which is a percentage of the amount you successfully raise. Check the platform's FAQs to find their fees. In addition to the platform's success fee, you can also expect credit card processing fees of approximately 3%.

   Crowdfunding platform's success fee = _____

   + Credit card processing fees = 3%

   = Total fees   _____

   If you're paying more than approximately 10% in total fees, then you might want to reassess the platform you've chosen and determine if they're offering value commensurate to their fees. Most platforms don't have fees beyond 7-8%. Once you've calculated the total fees, go back and include them in your total project costs. Go back to the section on *Determining Your Project Costs* to ensure that you've calculated and included these fees correctly.

3. **Are you familiar with some of the features that differentiate certain crowdfunding platforms?**

   Yes

   Perfect! Make sure the platform you choose has the features and benefits you need to run a successful campaign.

   No

   Not all portals and platforms are the same. Use the list and description of differentiating features below to help you decide which features you'll need to execute a successful campaign. This is not a complete or exhaustive list of all features, but highlights some of the more differentiated features. New features are being added all the time, so check the platform for a current assessment of their available features.

Feature	Description	Examples of platforms with feature available
All or nothing crowdfunding	No raised funds are awarded unless the entire fundraising goal is met. For example, if you seek to raise $10,000 and you only raise $9,500, all pledged funds return to the crowd and you receive nothing.	Kickstarter, Vovation
Crowd Knowledge	A crowdsourcing feature that allows the crowd to share their comments and ideas about a project	Vovation

Flexible/Keep what you raise	All funds raised are available even if the goal isn't reached	Indiegogo, RocketHub, GoFundMe
Google Analytics	Monitor page traffic with existing Google analytics account	Indiegogo
Team members	Provide team members access to log-in to your campaign dashboard and edit, update, etc.	IndieGoGo
Tipping point Tilting point	Allows for two fundraising milestones: the tipping or tilting point and an ultimate goal	StartSomeGood Tilt

4. **Be aware of the potential lag times before launch and after a successful raise on some platforms.**
   If you're planning to crowdfund on Kickstarter, make sure you set-up your account 7-10 days before your anticipated launch date. This is advice John Scaletta of Motion Source Video wish he knew before launching his crowdfunding campaign on Kickstarter. According to Scaletta, it was a hassle to get his Amazon Payments account set up and have his project manually approved by Kickstarter[32].

   In addition, some platforms have lag times after you've successfully raised funds. Make sure you're prepared to wait 2-3 weeks to receive your funds after a successful campaign just in case. I was a part of a small crowdfunding campaign to raise $6,000 to start a photo booth business. The funds successfully raised through the crowdfunding campaign were needed to pay for manufacturing the booth. It was supposed to be built and proudly displayed during the launch party after the campaign ended. When the disbursement of funds from IndieGoGo was delayed by more than two weeks, it caused a lot of unforeseen problems in our planned timeline. Fortunately, interim funding became available and the launch party was a success.

   IndieGoGo has since improved this lag time and when I finished up another campaign with them more than a year later, we only had to wait about 2 business days to receive funds, but this may not be the case with all crowdfunding platforms.

5. **Which platform will you choose?**
   If you're still unsure which platform to choose, you can conduct some research using a comprehensive directory of platforms on crowdsourcing.org:
   http://www.crowdsourcing.org/directory

---

[32] Scaletta, John. The Advice We Wish We Heard Before Crowdfunding On Kickstarter. 24 Dec. 2013 <http://www.crowdfundinsider.com/2013/12/28905-advice-wish-heard-crowdfunding-kickstarter/?utm_source=News+Update+Subscribers&utm_campaign=dcf91fb908-RSS_EMAIL_CAMPAIGN&utm_medium=email&utm_term=0_f649e5a188-dcf91fb908-17337245>

We've also includes some additional information and special tips for specific platforms below:

IndieGoGo

IndieGoGo is probably the most encompassing crowdfunding platform out there; meaning you can crowdfund anything and everything on their site with few categorical or even geographic restrictions. This can be a good thing or bad thing depending on how you look at it. For many, it means the freedom to fund any idea – as weird or ambitious as you can imagine, but for others it can feel like your project is lost in a swath of other initiatives. One way IndieGoGo has tried to overcome this is through their Gogofactor.

Gogofactor: A mathematical algorithm that determines which crowdfunding campaigns get featured on IndieGoGo within a specific category or on IndieGoGo's home page, as well as which projects are chosen for IndieGoGo's marketing or press. "It's a meritocracy, so the harder you work, the more likely your Gogofactor will go up and that's [when IndieGoGo] can help to amplify your campaign." [33]

Although the specifics of this algorithm are kept secret, the determinant variables include (in no specific or verified order of importance):

- How often you update your crowdfunding page.
- How often you share your campaign.
- How often you update your fans and funders
- How many people have visited your campaign page.
- How many contributions you have received.
- How many dollars raised.

Source: IndieGoGo

---

[33] Labovitz, Erica. IndieGoGo Director of Marketing interview with Carl Esposti. 11 Dec, 2011.
http://www.crowdsourcing.org/editorial/carl-esposti-interviews-erica-labovitz-of-crowdfunding-site-indiegogo-video/9109

Kickstarter

If you were familiar with the term 'crowdfunding' before reading this guide, you were also almost certainly familiar with the crowdfunding platform, _Kickstarter_. Indeed, Kickstarter has become synonymous with crowdfunding – what the Kleenex brand is to facial tissue. Kickstarter is the 200 pound gorilla of crowdfunding.

Since its founding in 2009, Kickstarter has made it possible for people to raise more than $1 billion for their projects[34]. The chart below shows the growth in the amount of dollars pledged to projects over a three year period from 2010-2013, a 177% average growth rate!

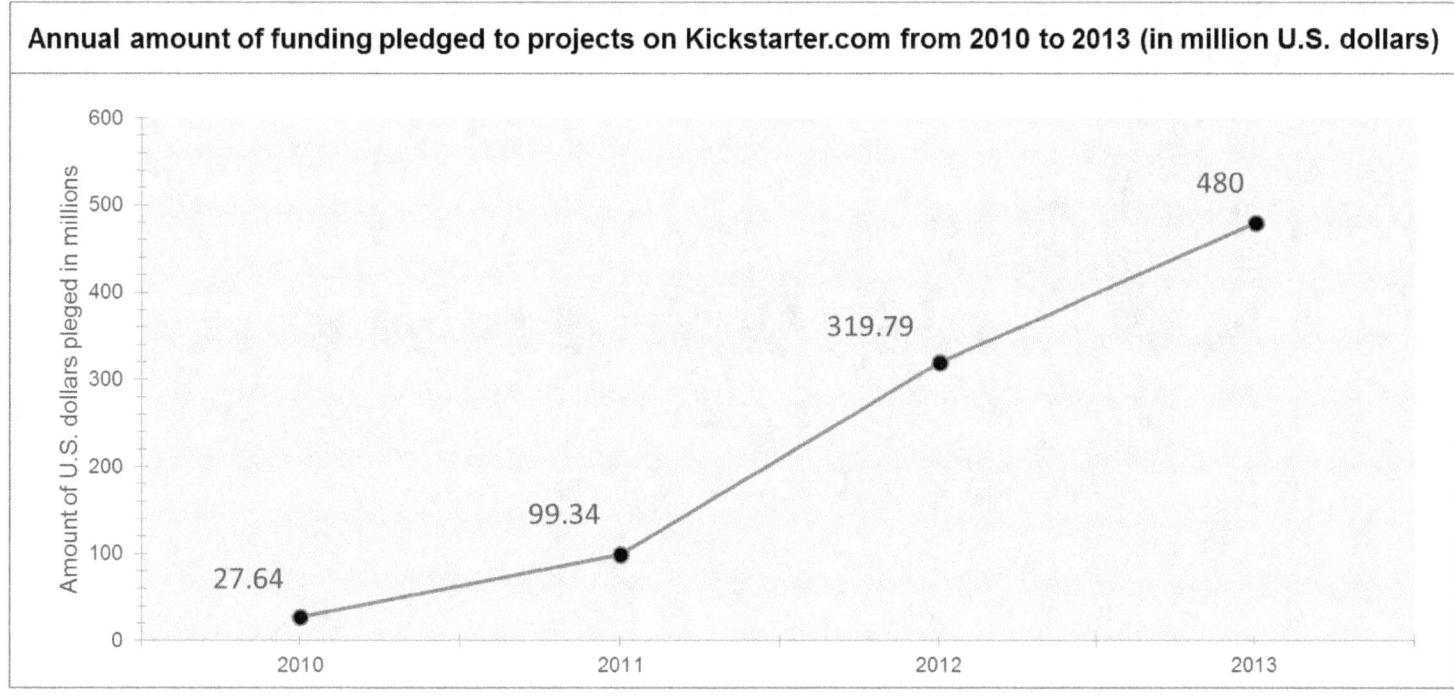

Annual amount of funding pledged to projects on Kickstarter.com from 2010 to 2013 (in million U.S. dollars)

Figure 6: Amount of funding pledged to projects on Kickstarter 2010-2013; Source: Kickstarter.com

---

[34] www.kickstarter.com/1billion

The chart below shows the number of successful projects on Kickstarter organized by category. The top five categories are music, film/video, art, publishing, and theatre[35]. If you're doing a project related to film or music, I highly recommend Kickstarter.

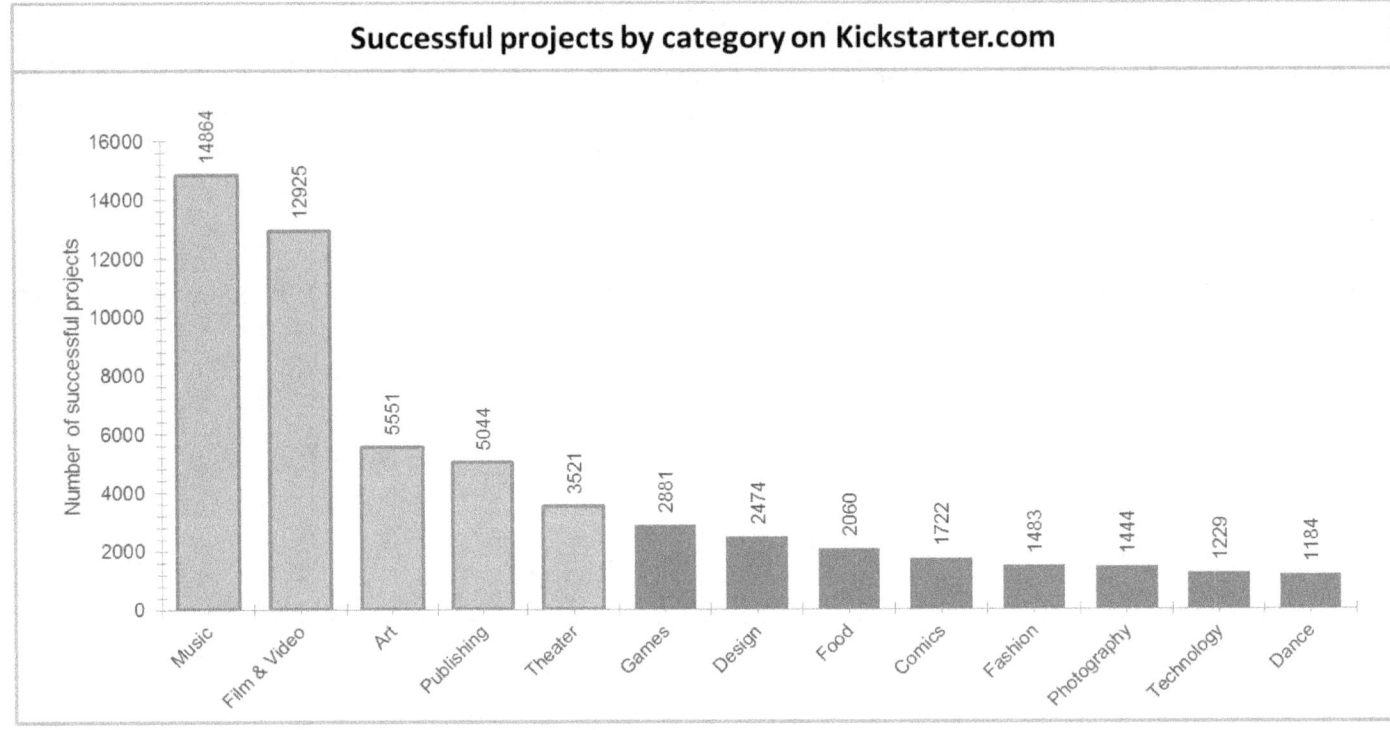

Figure 7: Successful Projects by Category on Kickstarter.com as of February, 2014

---

[35] Statista. February, 2014. Data source Kickstarter.com

Notes:

_____

_____

_____

_____

_____

_____

REV Up Your Network

 Crowdfunding is revolutionary because it offers relatively few barriers to accessing capital for a new and unproven product, service offering or project. However, substantial social capital is needed to be successful. It's imperative that your network be large enough and engaged enough to support your project.

In earlier sections we touched on how to determine project costs, enhance your online presence and the overall importance of a strong network, especially those that will contribute early to a campaign. Use the assessment below to ensure your network is REV'd up and ready to support your campaign.

1. **Will your 1st level network (family and close friends or colleagues) provide the social proof your campaign needs to be successful?**

One of the most common mistakes I see with unsuccessful crowdfunding campaigns is that they failed to provide social proof early on. Social proof signals to potential contributors outside of your immediate network that you have a project worthy of their money.

Earlier we said that your 1st level network should be able to fund approximately 25%-33% of your project, but to obtain social proof, you need your family and close friends to contribute some of that, at least 10% - 15% of your total raise, within the first 24-48 hours of your campaign launch. In fact, a campaign's probability of success increases by 100% after the first contribution is made and 400% after reaching 10% of the fundraising goal[36].

The chart below shows the number of unsuccessful campaigns on Kickstarter by the total amount raised. Approximately 69,000 unsuccessful campaigns raised less than 20% of the total fundraising goal. However, as you can see from the linear trend line, once a campaign raises more than 20% of its fundraising goal, the chances of success greatly increase. Only 19% of all unsuccessful campaigns fail after raising more than 20% of the fundraising goal.

> ## Social proof
>
> *Social proof, in the context of crowdfunding, refers to the credibility provided by early contributions to a campaign, signaling to others outside of the closest network circle (family and close friends) that the project and its claims are legitimate.*

---

[36] "Crowdfunding's Potential for the Developing World". 2013. Information for Development Program (InfoDev), Finance and Private Sector Development Department. Washington, DC: World Bank.

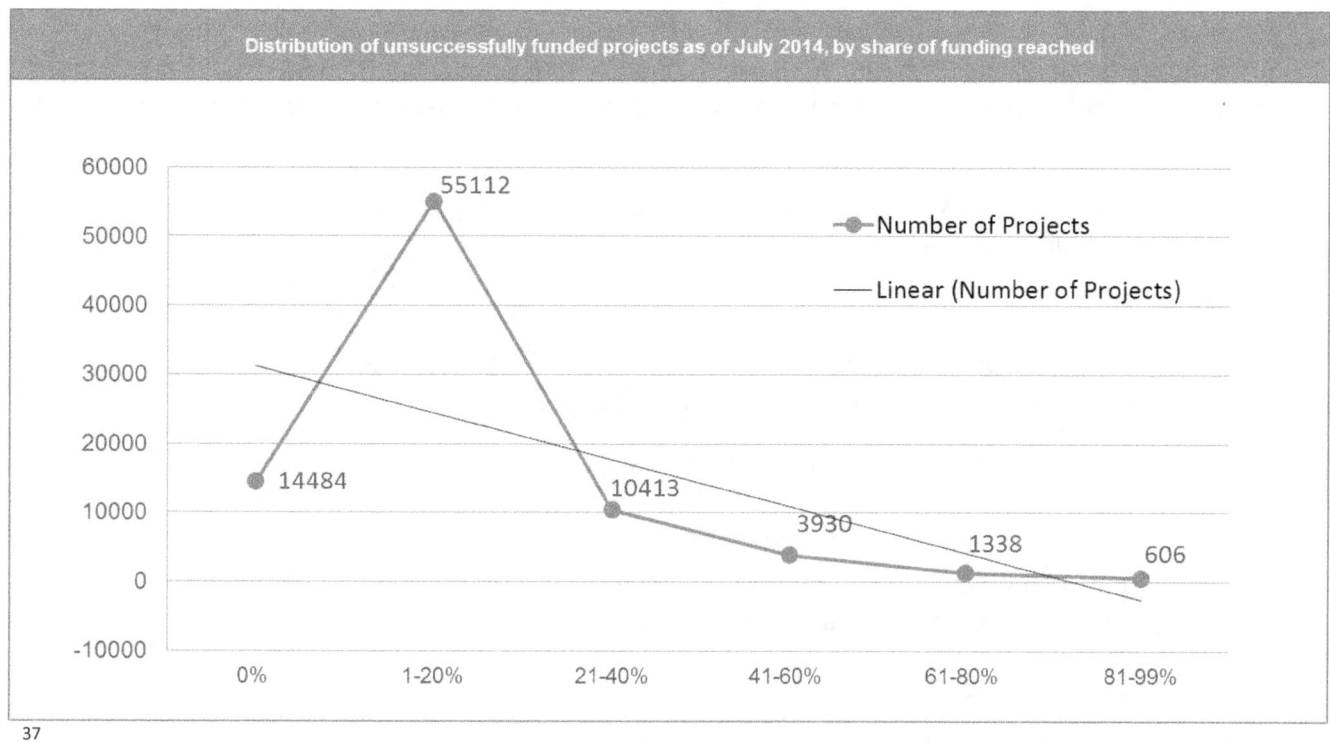

Distribution of unsuccessfully funded projects as of July 2014, by share of funding reached

37

This is why it's so important to obtain social proof through early contributions from your 1st level network. So, as a measurable goal, try to obtain 12-15 contributions from close friends and family before announcing your campaign to the public. If you can accomplish this, you'll be 74% more likely to reach your goal[38].

By nature, we're social creatures and learn by observing and following other's behavior. These initial funds are critical because no one outside of your immediate network (2nd and 3rd level networks) is likely to be the first contributor. However, they might become a follower and help you create a larger crowd of supporters.

Yes

Wonderful! Talk with them in person, call them, email or even Facebook message them letting them know that their contribution is needed within the first 24-48 hours of the campaign. Give them as much notice as you can so they're not surprised.

Also, set the expectation that you need them to fund at least 10%-15% immediately and have at least 10%-15% ready to contribute throughout the campaign if a project stalls or needs last minute funding to reach the goal.

No

Social proof is absolutely critical for a successful crowdfunding campaign. Without it, you'll be promoting an unexciting campaign that shows $0.00 raised. People want to be part of an exciting

[37] Kickstarter. July, 2014. Statista, 2014.
[38] Gray, Krista. Crowdtilt. 06/20/2014

campaign with momentum already established. If they see $0.00 raised, they will likely leave your project page and might never return. However, if they see that your campaign has already raised at least 10-15% of the total project amount in just a few days, they are more likely to contribute and sustain that early momentum.

If you are unable to obtain social proof for your crowdfunding campaign, you might be wise to reconsider launching until you can.

Unsure

Answer the following questions to help you assess whether or not your close friends and family will be able to provide the social proof you need for a successful campaign.

---

    a.   How much is 10%-15% of your project costs?

    _____

    b.   How many close friends and family members can you call upon to support your campaign early and provide social proof?

    _____

Now, divide your project cost by the number of close friends and family you can ask to provide social proof.

10-15% of total project costs ÷ # of close friends and family to provide social proof = _____

    c.   Does the amount calculated sound like a reasonable amount of money to expect, on average, from each one of your close friends and family members?

Now that you have answered these questions and completed these calculations, you should be better prepared to answer question 1 in this section.

2. When will you announce the launch of your campaign on social media?

It's imperative that you announce your campaign on social media and through PR outlets <u>only after you've obtained the social proof</u> described in the question above. Do not announce your campaign outside of your close circle of friends and family until you've received at least 10% of your total funding goal. Use the best practices below to guide you in your campaign announcement on social media.

Consider announcing your campaign on a weekend, where Facebook posts receive, on average, 14.5% higher rates of engagement[39]. If for some reason, announcing on the weekend doesn't mesh well with your campaign timeline, it's okay to post during other days of the week, but as a

---

[39] "Strategies for Effective Wall Posts: A Timeline Analysis". Pg 5. Sep. 2012. Salesforce. Marketing Cloud. Accessed 26 November 2013. http://www.salesforcemarketingcloud.com/wp-content/uploads/2013/03/Strategies-for-effective-wall-posts.pdf?1763e5

rule of thumb try to avoid Wednesdays, as it is found to have one of the lowest rates of engagement on Facebook.

Date of campaign launch announcement on social media: _____*

*Add this date to your crowdfunding campaign calendar under social media tasks.

3. **Who will you ask to share your posts, tweets, updates, etc?**

One of the least popular interactions on Facebook is sharing posts; likes and comments are a much more popular form of engagement. However, getting friends to share your posts, especially the announcement of your campaign is very important. You cannot rely on just posting and expecting someone to share your posts. You're going to have to ask people specifically to share your posts on their wall. Besides the campaign advocate or team you've identified and reached out to already, you'll also want to identify connections that you can ask to help pulsate your posts beyond your normal reach. Identify at least 10 connections below who you will ask to share your posts:

Connections that will share your posts, tweets, updates, etc.

Click to tweet is a free service that makes it easy to imbed a call to action for your blog readers to easily tweet a message or quote within your blog or newsletter. Simply compose the message you want tweeted by readers (see below) and then click "generate new link".

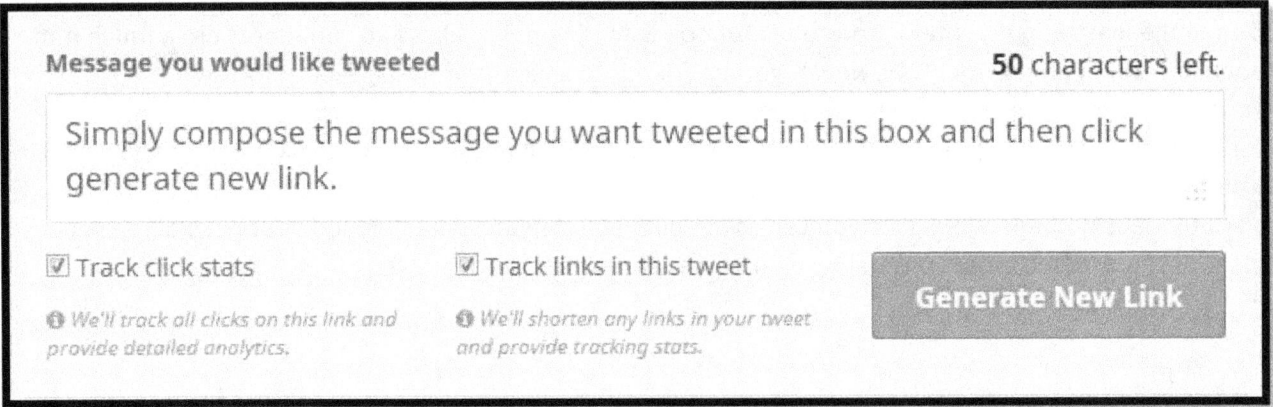

You can then imbed the link in your blog post or imbed it within a twitter icon/image (see below).

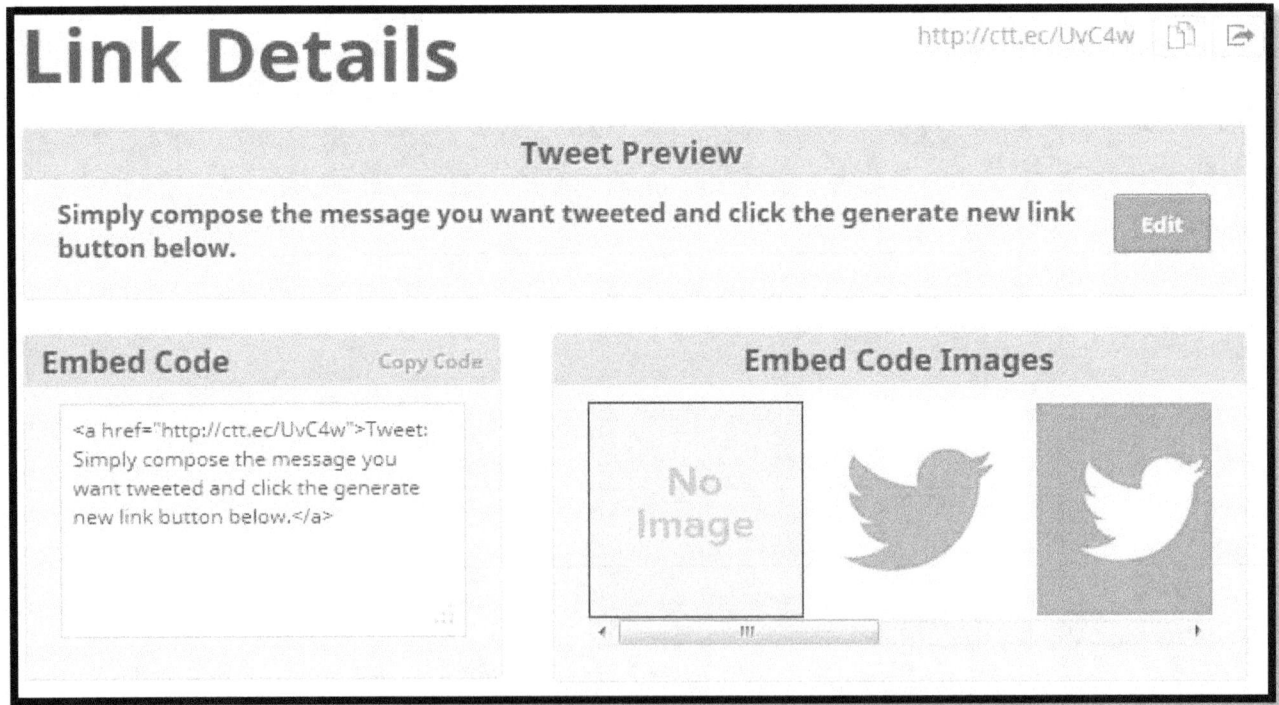

When a blog reader clicks the link to tweet, the message will be auto generated ready to share. This makes tweeting a quote in your blog super easy for readers.

4. When will you post, share, tweet updates about your campaign?

It's important to keep your network engaged and updated. In fact, campaign managers that provide updates throughout their campaign are approximately 26% more likely to successfully reach their fundraising goal[40]. With that said, you don't want to saturate them with too many posts and updates. So, as a rule of thumb, don't post more than 1-2 times per day and no more than 7 times in a week[41].

It's also a good idea to provide progress reports at spaced out intervals. For example, you might send out a progress report to backers that have already contributed, as well as potential funders once a week during the campaign. Update your crowdfunding campaign calendar with the dates you will post, share, tweet, blog, etc.

A great tool to help you coordinate your posts is Headtalker...

Helpful Resource: Headtalker

Headtalker is a unique resource that allows you to amplify and coordinate your message across a variety of social media platforms at a pre-determined time. Here's how it works:

1. Connect with your existing social media account
2. Create your crowdspeaking campaign by creating your message and determining when you want that message to go out.
3. Ask others in your network to pledge their support for your message by connecting their social media networks (Facebook, Twitter, LinkedIn, etc.) to your crowdspeaking campaign.
4. With enough support, you will reach your goal and your message will be automatically blasted through all of your supporters' connected social media networks.

5. Are you directly asking your network of friends and family to support you?

Yes

---

[40] Xu, Anbang; Yang, Xiao; Rao, Huaming; Fu, Wai-Tat; Huang, Shih-Wen; Bailey, Brian. "Show me the Money! An Analysis of Project Updates during Crowdfunding Campaigns". 2014
[41] "Strategies for Effective Wall Posts: A Timeline Analysis". Pg 15. Sep. 2012. Salesforce. Marketing Cloud. Accessed 26 November 2013. http://www.salesforcemarketingcloud.com/wp-content/uploads/2013/03/Strategies-for-effective-wall-posts.pdf?1763e5

Good. The advice I hear over and over again from successful crowdfunders is that they made direct asks to their friends and family with personal emails, messages, phone calls and even in person.

No

It's a humbling thing to do; asking someone directly to make a financial contribution toward your vision can be difficult and feel awkward for some people. However, if you want to make your vision a reality using crowdfunding capital, you must make those direct asks.

Don't just blast to the Facebook feed and say "check out my campaign". Instead, send people a personal message. Ask them how they've been. If you haven't spoken to them in a while, apologize and segue into discussing your project. It may seem specious, but it's all about how you frame it – this might even be a way to reignite an old friendship. Remember, you're not panhandling – you actually have a project that will benefit others, so you're not asking for yourself, you're simply the conduit to make something great happen.

Helpful Resource: Direct ask email message

Here is a sample email from our Community Loan Center crowdfunding campaign:

Hello _____,

How are you? I hope the new job is going well for you.

I'm messaging you because my organization is hard at work trying to create a viable alternative to predatory payday lending with the community loan center of Texas. To help raise awareness around our efforts and create the initial loan pool, we've launched a crowdfunding campaign on Indiegogo http://igg.me/at/communityloancenter/x/6944880

You can watch our video on that page to learn more about the program. I'm hoping you would consider donating $10 toward our efforts and sharing with your network. I'm reaching out to you because I know you're a great community ambassador, especially when it comes to fair lending practices and we really appreciate your support. Thank you for your consideration of this request and any help you're able to offer. I hope all is well.

Respectfully,

Lance McNeill

Notes:

_____

_____

_____

_____

_____

Fulfillment

This section of the guide is designed to help you after the fundraising period has ended. If you're reading this section, it's because you've successfully reached your funding goal, so congratulations! Now, it's time to take care of fulfillment. Fulfillment is about upholding the obligations you made during the campaign, delivering those perks and rewards you promised, and appropriating the funds raised toward their intended purpose in order to take the project beyond just an idea.

1. **Will you be shipping any perks/rewards internationally?**

   Yes

   Okay, hopefully you've passed along most of those shipping costs to the contributor. You'll also want to be sure that there aren't any import duties or taxes on your item. A free Import Duty and Taxes Calculator from DutyCalculator.com is a helpful resource for determining any taxes or import duties you may owe.

   No

   Great, you can skip to the next question.

   Helpful Resource: Import Duty and Taxes Calculator: http://www.dutycalculator.com/new-import-duty-and-tax-calculation/

   Helpful Resource: USPS Postage Price Calculator (http://ircalc.usps.gov/)

2. **Have you reached out to your backers to tell them thank you and let them know what to expect next?**

   Yes

   Wonderful, these are your early adopters – those that believed in you first – so make them feel like they're your best friends.

   No

   You're probably very busy, but take some time to draft a thoughtful email thanking those that just contributed to make your dream possible.

3. **Have you experienced any delays in receiving your funds?**

Yes

Okay, there are two potential bottlenecks that could delay funding. The first is with the crowdfunding portal. We waited for 15 business to receive our funds from IndieGoGo. It might have been longer had we not bugged them every other day with a barrage of email inquiries. Indiegogo has since expedited their payment processing, but if you're experiencing any issues, it's time to be a squeaky wheel and find out when you will receive your funding.

The second bottleneck can come from the payment gateways. This one is a little trickier. Popular payment processors like PayPal and WePay are responsible for chargebacks from credit card companies. A chargeback happens when a card holder disputes a charge on his or her account. This is a common occurrence when a cardholder complains about not receiving the products or services they paid for. This is why it's extremely important to keep your backers updated and set realistic expectations and timelines for them.

To avoid chargebacks, some payment gateways are delaying the release of funds until they're reassured that the perks/rewards will be delivered[42]. This is because these gateways are responsible for paying back the cardholder even if they've already released the funds to the seller (crowdfunder). This is more likely to occur with campaigns that have raised a significant amount of money. The best thing to do if you find yourself in this situation is to contact the payment gateway (PayPal, WePay, etc.) directly and tell them more about yourself and your crowdfunding campaign. Reassure them that you are going to fulfill those perk/reward orders and that you're not a fraudulent outfit. Be respectful, but direct in your correspondence. Best of luck.

No

Great, you're good to go!

4. Share your story

It's important to share your story and keep the buzz going about your project. For various reasons, many media outlets have moratoriums on crowdfunding stories while a campaign is live, but they may be willing to do a story about a successful crowdfunding campaign. Reach out to your local and relevant media outlets and let them know you've been successful in raising funds.

Notes:

_____

_____

_____

_____

_____

_____

_____

_____

---

[42] Luzar, Charles. "Crowdfunding and What you Should Know About Online Payments Before Luanch". 4 March. 2014. Crowdfund Insider <http://www.crowdfundinsider.com/2014/03/32400-crowdfunders-need-make-sure-get-paid/?utm_source=News+Update+Subscribers&utm_campaign=4dd6c0fc46-RSS_EMAIL_CAMPAIGN&utm_medium=email&utm_term=0_f649e5a188-4dd6c0fc46-17337245>

Crowdfunding Project's Mission Statement Worksheet

Instructions:
Answer the following questions about your project and use the answers to draft a Mission Statement.

What is the project's name or working title?

_____

Why are we pursuing this project; what do we do/what is our purpose? What do we want to accomplish?
Consider starting with prepositional phrases, such as "to promote," "dedicated to," "committed to", "devoted to," etc.

_____

_____

_____

_____

Who are our customers or clients? Who is our target market? Who are we trying to reach? Who will benefit from our product or service?

_____

_____

_____

How will we differentiate our project and be successful? What is our business model? What is our greatest strength? How will we achieve success and set ourselves a part from others doing similar projects?

_____

_____

_____

_____

What are our values? What do we believe in? What are our responsibilities to the community?

_____

_____

_____

Example Mission Statements:

Example 1:

Foundation Communities' Small Business Coaching Program is dedicated to empowering self-employed clients and small business owners with the knowledge and tools they need to reach their entrepreneurial aspirations.

Through one-on-one coaching and classroom style instruction we aim to establish the foundation our clients need to build capacity in their own self-sufficient path toward success.

Example 2:
Civic Square is committed to increasing civic engagement, participation and collaboration in pursuit of a more democratic society, one community at a time.

Example 3:
Keep Austin Funded is a self-sustaining social enterprise committed to providing local entrepreneurs with the knowledge, tools, and ultimately, access to crowdfunding capital in a comprehensive platform that empowers and enables their success.

SMART goals are Specific, Measurable, Attainable, Realistic and Timely, separated into the short-term (goals you will have accomplished in the next 3-6 months), medium-term (goals you will have accomplished in the next 6-24 months) and long-term (goals you will have accomplished in the next 2-5 years). Note that we're not setting goals beyond five years with this exercise. You should revisit your goals every 6-12 months and set new ones for the horizon. Scenario planning, which is not addressed in this worksheet, is a better method to use for projects that require planning beyond 5 years.

Examples:

Unspecific Goal: Hire employees

Specific Goal: Hire one part-time marketing employee

Unmeasurable Goal: Increase sales

Measurable goal: Increase sales by 25%

Unattainable goal: Increase lead conversion rate by 2,000% in the next month

Attainable goal: Increase lead conversion rate by 5% next month

Unrealistic goal: Capture 10% market share in our first year of operations

Realistic goal: Capture 1-2% market share in our first year

Untimely goal: Expand to a second location

Timely goal: Expand to a second location during year 3.

Specific
Measurable
Attainable
Realistic
Timely

SMART goals:

- Within the next 3 months, file for a federal trademark.
- By 6 months, reach $25,000 in total sales
- Within 1 year, hire a part-time employee, intern or virtual assistant to assist with social media marketing for 15-20 hours per week.
- By year 3, expand from the farmer's market to a food trailer
- By year 5, open up a retail location in East Austin.

Now, use the SMART goal template on the following pages to create your S.M.A.R.T goals:

- Short-term goals are 5-10 goals that can be accomplished in the next 3-6 months.
- Medium-term goals are 3-5 goals that can be accomplished in the next 6-24 months.
- Long-term goals are 1-3 goals that can be accomplished in the next 2-5 years.

Short-term Goals (to accomplish in the next 3-6 months)

- _____

  _____

  _____

- _____

  _____

  _____

- _____

  _____

  _____

- _____

  _____

  _____

- _____

  _____

  _____

- _____

  _____

  _____

- _____

  _____

  _____

Medium-term Goals (to accomplish in the next 6-24 months)

- _____
  _____
  _____
- _____
  _____
  _____
- _____
  _____
  _____
- _____
  _____
  _____
- _____
  _____
  _____

Long-term Goals (to accomplish in the next 2-5 years, no longer)

- _____

_____

_____

- _____

_____

_____

- _____

_____

_____

Project Cost Template

Use the template below to estimate your project costs. After you've itemized your costs, I recommend you include a small cushion of 5%-10% for miscellaneous or unexpected costs.

	Per unit costs	Quantity	Tax	Total costs
Advertising & Marketing				
Business cards				
Direct mail				
Online advertising				
Printed promo materials				
Website development				
Web domain & hosting				
Furniture, Fixtures and Equipment				
Computer/printer/hardware				
Equipment rental/lease				
Furniture				
machinery				
Security system				
Bank charges and fees				
Business Insurance				
Business interruption				
Fire/theft/flood				
Inventory insurance				
Liability, malpractice, errors & omissions				
Worker's comp				
Business Loan Interest				
Communication Utilities				
Cell phone				
Internet				
Telephone				
Crowdfunding fees				
Education				
conferences/conventions				
courses/lessons/workshops				
Legal & Professional Services				
Accounting fees				
Legal fees				
Consulting fees				
Licenses & Fees				
Business license				
Entity formation fees				
Permits				
Copyright/royalty/patent				
Office Supplies				

Office materials				
Cleaning supplies				
Coffee, water, snacks				
software				
Postage and Delivery (shipping)				
Rent/lease on property				
Repairs/Maintenance				
Supplies in Cost of Goods Sold (COGS)				
Taxes				
Payroll taxes				
Franchise tax				
Business property tax				
Transportation				
Travel				
Meals & Entertainment				
Membership dues/fees				
Publications				
Books				
Industry journals				
Digital subscriptions				
Utilities				
Electricity				
Pest control				
security service				
Gas				
Water/waste water				
Waste removal				
Misc. or contingency				
Business gifts				
Uniforms				
Wages/salary to employees				

Total Project Costs	0

Owner's contribution	
Investor(s) contribution	
crowdfunding contribution	
bank loan	
Total Contributions	0

Examples of 100+ Business Expenses

Below is a list of 100+ common business expenses provided by June Walker, author of multiple tax advice publications designed for independent professionals and small business owners.

June Walker

4 Montana Court • Santa Fe, NM 87508
indie@junewalkeronline.com • 877.666.5144

After you have visited my website www.junewalkeronline.com and read Is it a deductible business expense? which explains what makes an expense a business deduction, the following list will be helpful in providing you with typical as well as not- so-typical examples of business expense deductions. There are about 100 posts on my blog that relate to specific business expenses. You might want to check them out. Or for a more in-depth explanation, check out my book The Confident Indie: A Simple Guide to Deductions, Income and Taxes for The Creatively Self-employed.

As I say in the book about maintaining an Indie Power Mindset, "anything you do that relates to your work, that stimulates or enhances your business, nurtures your professional creativity, improves your skills, wins you recognition, or increases your chances of making a sale may be a business expense and therefore deductible." If you maintain your indie power mindset you needn't worry about missing any potential business deduction.

If you have a question about a specific deduction please email your question to me at

indie@junewalkeronline.com and I'll do my best to get to it help you.

If you *know* that an expense is deductible, don't concern yourself with which expense category it fits into. Simply categorize it to the closest match you can find or give the expense its own category name and deduct it. The IRS will not disallow the deduction for being in the wrong category as long as it is a legitimate expense.

Note that the order of expense categories listed below is similar to the order on the federal tax form, Schedule C: Profit or Loss from Business.

EXAMPLES OF 100+ BUSINESS EXPENSES

Advertising / Promotion

- Business Cards
- Christmas / Holiday Cards
- Google Ads
- Mailing Lists
- Photo Production
- Posters
- Professional Registries
- Resumes
- Webinars - that promote you or your business
- Website Development & Hosting

Auto / Truck / Motorcycle: On the AUTO worksheet (see website)

Commissions / Fees
- Agent Fees
- Franchise Fees

Subcontractor Fees

- Assistant
- Business Coach
- Models
- Supervision for Psychologists
- Voice Coach

Equipment: Costs more than $100 and lasts more than one year

- Office Furniture / Lamps
- Computer / Printer / Scanner / All Technical Hardware
- Washer / Dryer: e.g. massage therapist business % for business linens
- Alarm System
- Camera & Accessories
- File Cabinets
- Music System
- Rugs
- SmartPhone
- Stand Alone Shelves

- TV & Video
- iPad

Business Insurance
- Business Interruption - for loss of profit due to fire, etc.
- Credit Coverage - for unpaid debts
- Disability for non-spousal employees only
- Fire / Theft / Flood
- Liability & Malpractice
- Merchandise & Inventory
- Workers' Compensation for Employees

Business Loan Interest
- Mortgage on Business Property
- Business Loan
- Business Portion of Credit Card Finance Charges

Legal & Professional Services: for business only, e.g. not will preparation
- Accountant Fees
- Attorney Fees
- Bookkeeper Fees
- Lobbying Expenses with Restrictions
- Pension Administrator Fees for Employees

Office Supplies & Expense: General supplies used in your office or workplace; note, fine art is not an office décor expense
- Office Materials: e.g. paper, toner, light bulbs
- Cleaning Supplies & Paper Products: e.g. tissues; towels
- Coffee / Bottled Water / Candy for The Office
- Fire Extinguisher
- Flowers / Plants for The Office
- Plant Hangers
- Software

Postage
- US Mail / Fed Ex / UPS
- Freight / Shipping
- Messenger Service
- Post Office Box: Business % if also used for personal

Equipment Rental / Lease
- Chairs
- Tables
- Workshop Tools

Rent On Business Property
- Office
- Studio
- Rehearsal Space
- Warehouse

Repairs / Maintenance
- Of Equipment: e.g. piano tuning; service contract
- Of The Office: e.g. cleaning service; repair of a window
- Laundering of Linens Used in Your Practice
- Landscaping / Lawn care for Business Property

Supplies: Incidental supplies used in your specific business, not office supplies and not supplies used in the production of your product
- Animal Treats for A Dog Sitter
- Linens for A Massage Therapist
- Music Scores for A Music Teacher
- Props & Scripts for A Performing Artist

Business Taxes
- Employer's Share Of Payroll Taxes
- Federal Highway Use Tax
- Franchise Tax
- Gross Receipts / Sales Tax
- NY Commuter Tax
- NY Unincorporated Business Tax
- Personal Property Tax on Business Assets
- Real Estate Tax on Business Property

Licenses / Fees
- Yearly Business License
- Franchise Fees
- Regulatory Fees to State & Local Governments
- Zoning Permit

Travel: On the TRAVEL worksheet (see junewalkeronline.com for worksheet)

Meals / Entertainment
- With Business Associates: e.g. clients, potential clients, colleagues, employees
- At Your Office
- At A Sporting Or Entertainment Event
- Parties for Business Associates
- For The General Public: e.g. for a grand opening or gallery show

Telephone & Other Communication Utilities
- Monthly Service + Accessories for Business Line
- Business % of Personal Line exclude base line charge
- Cell or Smartphone Service
- Answering Service
- Internet Service Provider

Office Or Studio Utilities: Not home office
- Electricity / Heat / Water / Trash Pick-up
- Exterminator Service
- Security company fees

Wages to Employees

Bank Services Charges: Allocate if both business and personal use

- Business Bank Account Fees
- Check Printing Fees
- Client Returned Check Fee
- Safe Deposit Box

Copyright Fees / Royalties / Patents
Costumes / Cleaning / Make-up
- Clothing with Business Name Permanently Attached or Printed
- Tuxedo / Evening Dress
- Hair Done for Award Presentation
- Make-up for A Performer
- Uniforms

Dues / Entrance Fees
- Civic & Public Service Organizations: e.g. chambers of commerce
- Competition Fees
- Professional Societies: e.g. bar or medical associations; real estate boards

Business Gifts: Maximum, $25 per person, per year
- To Clients
- To Potential Clients
- To Business Associates
- Thank You to Mom for Fixing Your Computer
- Tips: e.g. for travel assistants; backstage help

Studio / Office-In-The-Home (see junewalkeronline.com for worksheet)
Publications / Anything you read
- Books
- Digital Subscriptions
- Kindle, Nook Downloads
- Online Research Services
- Newspapers & Magazines ... if they're still around in hardcopy

Recording Costs
- Master
- Packaging
- Production
- Recording Studio
- Studio Musicians
- Studio Techs

Study / Education / Seminars / Research
- Concerts
- Conventions
- ISP
- Lessons / Courses
- Library Fee
- Museums / Galleries
- Performances
- Tuition & Fees
- Video / Film / DVDs: attend / purchase / rental a la Netflix

- Webinars
- Workshops

Transportation
- Bus
- Subway / Train
- Taxi

Supplies Used in the Production of Your Product

Crowdfunding Campaign Action Plan   **Date:** _____

Goal(s):   **1.**_____

               2._____

               3._____

Action Steps *What needs to be accomplished?*	Responsibilities *Who is responsible for accomplishing it?*	Deadline *By when?*	Resources *Resources required to accomplish task (financial, human, technological, etc.)*	Notes
Step 1:			A. B.	
Step 2:			A. B.	
Step 3:			A. B.	
Step 4:			A. B.	
Step 5:			A. B.	

Turning Social Capital into Start-up Capital™

Network Reach

Network Reach	Current Level	Goal	Suggestions
Friends on Personal Facebook account?			10 FB friends = 9% chance of success 100 FB friends = 20% chance of success 1000 FB friends = 40% chance of success Join new social networks and expand existing ones.
Likes on Business Facebook account?			Be sure to create a Business Facebook page to improve your credibility
Followers on Personal Twitter?			
Followers on Business Twitter?			Find the leading bloggers in your field and follow them on Twitter
Connections on LinkedIn?			Become members of any industry related groups on LinkedIn
#Meetup Groups you're a member of?			Look for local groups you can join to learn and spread the word
#Meetup Groups you attend monthly?			Increase the # of groups you attend monthly for maximum exposure
Other Social Media Networks?			Look for other online communities to share with
How many professional associations are you a member of?			
How many subscribe to your newsletter			
How frequently do you blog?			
How often do you tweet?			
How many in your network would contribute $'s to your project?			Expand your network and start talking about your project
Do you have a web presence?			Have a website or landing page to promote your crowdfunding projects and provide credibility to yourself

Perks/Rewards Idea List

These 50 perk/reward ideas were obtained from various successful projects on Kickstarter.com and Indiegogo.com. You can search these sites using the provided project name for more information. In order from left to right, this list shows the amount being asked for the perk/reward, a short description of the perk/reward, the general industry the project is related to, more specifically what the project is, the number of backers who contributed funds for that particular perk/reward, the percentage of those backers compared to all the backers of the project, the total number of project backers, the name of the project, the total amount raised and finally any interesting notes about the project.

Project Name	Project type	Perk	Contribution level for perk	Total raised from perk	Total project funds raised	# of backers	Notes
Foodie Dice: Play with your food	kitchenware	Shipping updates	$1.00	$28.00	$135,000.00	28	
Simple diaper & linen	laundry services	Good karma	$5.00	$80.00	$12,215.00	16	
Zego bars	energy bars	sampler	$10.00	$820.00	$50,239.00	82	food allergy friendly energy bars
Good Spread Peanut Butter	peanut butter	Name on founders page/wall	$10.00	$330.00	$69,518.00	33	
Tom Zuba's Permission to Mourn	educational book	Drawing & thank you	$10.00	$90.00	$22,806.00	9	Thank you & drawing for 2 autographed copies of the book
Foodie Dice: Play with your food	kitchenware	Earlybird Product	$12.00	$300.00	$135,000.00	25	
Foodie Dice: Play with your food	kitchenware	Product	$16.00	$2,832.00	$135,000.00	177	
Tom Zuba's Permission to Mourn	educational book	Loved one's name in book	$20.00	$660.00	$22,806.00	33	The name of your loved one will be written in a tribute page in the book and on their website

Project Name	Project type	Perk	Contribution level for perk	Total raised from perk	Total project funds raised	# of backers	Notes
Simple diaper & linen	laundry services	swag: bumper sticker	$25.00	$725.00	$12,215.00	29	
Omaha Bicycle Co.	bike shop	Swag: Pint glass	$25.00	$325.00	$15,041.00	13	
Napa Bookmine	bookstore	Swag: tote bag	$25.00	$1,275.00	$17,035.00	51	
Blackberry Market	market retail	mini-cupcake sampler	$25.00	$250.00	$26,226.00	10	
Good Spread Peanut Butter	peanut butter	Product & recipe book	$25.00	$9,150.00	$69,518.00	366	
Restaurant expansion	restaurant	$25 gets you $50 in food	$25.00	$2,050.00	$34,886.00	82	restaurant expanding into larger space
in.gredients	grocery retail	reusable container	$25.00	$2,650.00	$15,455.00	106	Austin's ingredients grocery store start-up funding
Foodie Dice: Play with your food	kitchenware	Product in specialized packaging	$26.00	$8,372.00	$135,000.00	322	
Restaurant expansion	restaurant	$50 gets you $100 in food	$50.00	$600.00	$34,886.00	12	restaurant expanding into larger space
Happy feet	flip flops	product	$50.00	$1,550.00	$15,110.00	31	
TRF Café L.O.V.E	café retail	10% off for a month + swag	$50.00	$4,100.00	$26,195.00	82	
Tutor Tango - online tutoring service	Tutoring	Signed book	$50.00	$650.00	$10,341.00	13	Offered a popular grammar book signed by author
Baker stove: energy efficient cookstove for developing world	Stove	Stove (extra early bird price)	$55.00	$2,750.00	$35,632.00	50	

Project Name	Project type	Perk	Contribution level for perk	Total raised from perk	Total project funds raised	# of backers	Notes
Zego bars	energy bars	24 energy bars	$60.00	$3,000.00	$50,239.00	50	2 boxes of energy bars
TRF Café L.O.V.E	café retail	Raw food class	$60.00	$900.00	$26,195.00	15	Raw food class teaching how to make raw vegan sushi and wasabi
Baker stove: energy efficient cookstove for developing world	Stove	Stove (Early bird price)	$63.00	$2,961.00	$35,632.00	47	
Michael Grey Footwear Debut line	footwear	Pair of flats	$65.00	$1,300.00	$10,780.00	20	
Forus	athletic shoes	Pair of athletic shoes	$70.00	$8,330.00	$48,198.00	119	10% of proceeds support their philanthropic mission
Samsung S4 Wireless Charger from WiQiQi	Cellular	Product + wordwide shipping	$72.00	$4,176.00	$16,857.00	58	
in.gredients	grocery retail	growler of local beer	$75.00	$1,650.00	$15,455.00	22	Austin's ingredients grocery store start-up funding
Move loot	moving	Launch Party + swag	$75.00	$675.00	$15,025.00	9	
Michael Grey Footwear Debut line	footwear	Pair of heels	$85.00	$1,955.00	$10,780.00	23	
Blackberry Market	market retail	breakfast basket + swag	$100.00	$3,800.00	$26,226.00	38	
New Cooking Studio	classes	Cooking class + e-books	$100.00	$1,800.00	$15,851.00	18	funding for a new cooking studio

Project Name	Project type	Perk	Contribution level for perk	Total raised from perk	Total project funds raised	# of backers	Notes
Launch Seattle Attic!	co-working space	Name on plaque	$100.00	$1,300.00	$7,564.00	13	A community workshop /maker's space for women
Help the Anchor Salon get under way	salon	Grand opening party ticket	$100.00	$4,000.00	$10,186.00	40	Launch party featuring live music, beverages & appetizers
Michael Grey Footwear Debut line	footwear	Pair of boots	$115.00	$2,070.00	$10,780.00	18	
Help the Anchor Salon get under way	salon	Stylist services	$125.00	$1,250.00	$10,186.00	10	Hair color services & scalp massage
Forus	athletic shoes	2 Pairs of athletic shoes	$130.00	$4,160.00	$48,198.00	32	10% of proceeds support their philanthropic mission
Michael Grey Footwear Debut line	footwear	Pair of boots and flats	$145.00	$1,885.00	$10,780.00	13	
build a community deck	market retail	dinner for 2	$150.00	$600.00	$16,291.00	4	Existing market/café building a new outside deck
Ektoplazm 2.0: next-level music distribution	Online music platform	Beta access to site	$180.00	$2,160.00	$30,708.00	12	
Michael Grey Footwear Debut line	footwear	3 pairs of shoes - entire ladies collection	$205.00	$1,025.00	$10,780.00	5	
The Wellness Collective	wellness	$500 in wellness services + 15% lifetime discount	$250.00	$1,250.00	$20,375.00	5	

Project Name	Project type	Perk	Contribution level for perk	Total raised from perk	Total project funds raised	# of backers	Notes
Restaurant expansion	restaurant	20% off entire bill for 1 year	$250.00	$1,750.00	$34,886.00	7	restaurant expanding into larger space
Simple diaper & linen	laundry services	1 week of service	$300.00	$300.00	$12,215.00	1	1 week of laundry services
Napa Bookmine	bookstore	Visit Napa	$500.00	$2,000.00	$17,035.00	4	A 2-night stay for 2 in Napa Valley at entrepreneurs' bungalow home.
LetsMeetAtJoes... collaborative scheduling	Software	Swag, access to software & inclusion on steering committee	$500.00	$4,000.00	$13,470.00	8	The steering committee allows you to help develop the product strategy
Bump water	specialty water	Dinner party	$600.00	$1,800.00	$16,950.00	3	specialty water targeting pregnant women
Blackberry Market	market retail	space rental for private dinner	$2,500.00	$2,500.00	$26,226.00	1	private dinner space rental of up to 12 guests
Fix Young America	Publication & Political organization	National Rally Organizer	$6,000.00	$12,000.00	$39,052.00	2	"A solutions based book & movement that aims to end youth unemployment..."

Perks & Rewards Example: Misty Dawn Documentary

The Misty Dawn Documentary tells the story of Misty, a victim of domestic violence. These are the perks and rewards drafted for their crowdfunding campaign.

	Perk/Reward Description	Total cost (including shipping)	Contribution Amount	Surplus
1	You'll receive good karma for your contribution and help to spread awareness about domestic violence	$0	$5.00	$5
2	You'll receive your name in the credits at the end of the documentary + good karma	$0	$10.00	$10
3	Misty Dawn Documentary Early Bird Price. (Limited to 10). Get a digital copy of the documentary + name in credits + good karma	$0	$20.00	$20
4	Misty Dawn Documentary. Get a digital copy of the documentary. + name in credits + good karma	$0	$25.00	$25
5	Misty Dawn Documentary DVD Early Bird Price. (Limited to 10) (U.S shipping included) + name in credits + good karma	$7	$35.00	$28
6	Misty Dawn Documentary DVD. (U.S Shipping included) + name in credits + good karma	$7	$40.00	$33
7	Invitation to an exclusive screening of the Misty Dawn Documentary + Misty Dawn Documentary (Digital or DVD) + name in credits + good karma	$7.00	$55.00	$48
8	A special thank you from the producer filmed and sent to you digitally + invitation to an exclusive screening of the Misty Dawn documentary + Misty Dawn documentary (digital or DVD) + name in credits + good karma	$7.00	$100.00	$93
9	Business sponsorship with business name and logo in the credits of the documentary + invitation to an exclusive screening of the documentary + Misty Dawn documentary (digital or DVD)	$7.00	$250.00	$243
10	Executive Producer Recognition in the credits + invitation to an exclusive screening of the Misty Dawn documentary + Misty Dawn documentary (digital or DVD)	$0.00	$500.00	$500

Perks & Rewards Worksheet

This worksheet is designed to help you organize and estimate the value of the various perks/rewards you will offer to backers/contributors. The first row is an example of a coffee mug offered as a "swag" perk/reward. I've completely estimated the costs of the mug, but for every perk/reward you will offer, you need to research the true costs. In my example, I've estimated the coffee mug itself will cost $1 and printing my logo on it will cost another $1. It's going to be relatively expensive to package and ship a coffee mug to backers; $1 for packaging and $2 for shipping. The total cost of my coffee mug perk is $5.

Not that you've calculated the cost, you need to put a "price" on it by deciding the level of contribution a backer will need to make to be eligible for the perk/reward. As a rule of thumb, the contribution level should be at least 3-4 times the cost of the reward. This is because you want to create a surplus to allocate back to the project costs.

The next column asks you to estimate the quantity of perks/rewards claimed. Be reasonable with your estimate, taking into consideration similar perks/rewards from the list provided earlier in the appendix. This estimate will help you determine if you have enough offerings to support the surplus necessary to fund your project. The next two columns are for calculating how much will be raised from the perk/reward and then, by subtracting the cost of the perk/reward, determine how much surplus will be available to fund your project.

	Perk/Reward Description	Total cost (including shipping)	Contribution Amount	Estimated Quantity	Total Raised	Surplus
1	Example: Coffee mug with logo + a special thank you on our facebook page	Mug = $1, printing = $1, Packaging = $1 shipping =$2 Total cost=$5	$20	10	contribution amount * estimated quantity of perk/reward = $200	$200 raised-(10 units*$5 cost per unit) = $150 surplus for the project
2						
3						

	Perk/Reward Description	Total Cost (Including Shipping)	Contribution Amount	Estimated Quantity	Total Raised	Surplus
4						
5						
6						
7						
Limited or Expiring Reward						
Mid-point or fresh Reward						

American holidays, celebrations and observances

Federal holidays

1. **New Year's Day**
2. **Martin Luther King, Jr. Day**
   Martin Luther King, Jr. Day is celebrated on the third Monday in January.
3. **Washington's Birthday**
   Washington's Birthday is observed on the third Monday of February in honor of George Washington. This date is commonly called Presidents' Day.
4. **Memorial Day**
   Memorial Day is observed the last Monday of May.
5. **Independence Day**
   Independence Day is July 4.
6. **Labor Day**
   Labor Day is the first Monday of September.
7. **Columbus Day**
   Columbus Day is a celebrated on the second Monday in October. The day commemorates October 12, 1492, when Italian navigator Christopher Columbus landed in the New World.
8. **Veterans Day**
   Veterans Day is celebrated on November 11.
9. **Thanksgiving Day**
   Thanksgiving Day is celebrated on the fourth Thursday in November.
10. **Christmas Day**
    Christmas Day is a celebrated on December 25.

Celebrations and observances

These are some of the most popular American celebrations and observances that occur every year.

1. **Groundhog Day**
   Groundhog Day is February 2 and has been celebrated since 1887.
2. **Valentine's Day**
   Valentine's Day is celebrated on February 14. The day was named after an early Christian martyr, and on Valentine's Day, Americans give presents like candy or flowers to the ones they love.
3. **Earth Day**
   Earth Day is observed on April 22. First celebrated in 1970 in the United States, it inspired national legislation such as the Clean Air and Clean Water Acts. Earth Day is designed to promote ecology, encourage respect for life on earth, and highlight concern over pollution of the soil, air, and water.
4. **Arbor Day**
   National Arbor Day was proclaimed as the last Friday in April by President Richard Nixon in 1970. A number of state Arbor Days are observed at other times of the year to coincide with the best tree planting weather. The observance began in 1872, when Nebraska settlers and homesteaders were urged to plant trees on the largely treeless plains.
5. **Easter**
6. **Cinco de Mayo**
   The annual celebration honors Mexican heritage.
7. **Mother's Day**
   Mother's Day is the second Sunday of May.
8. **Flag Day**
   Flag Day, celebrated June 14, has been a presidentially proclaimed observance since 1916. Although Flag Day is not a federal holiday, Americans are encouraged to display the flag outside their homes and businesses on this day to honor the history and heritage the American flag represents.
9. **Father's Day**
   Father's Day celebrates fathers every third Sunday of June.
10. **Patriot Day**
    September 11, 2001, was a defining moment in American history. On that day, terrorists hijacked four commercial airliners to strike targets in the United States. Patriot Day and National Day of Service and Remembrance is observed on September 11 in honor of the victims of these attacks.
11. **Halloween**
    Halloween is celebrated on October 31.
12. **Pearl Harbor Day**
    Pearl Harbor Remembrance Day is December 7. In 1994, Congress designated this national observance to honor the more than 2,400 military service personnel who died on this date in 1941, during the surprise attack on Pearl Harbor, Hawaii, by Japanese forces.

Source: (http://www.usa.gov/citizens/holidays.shtml)

Introduction narrative

Introduce yourself and the project. The introduction should be no longer than 15-20 seconds.

_____

_____

_____

_____

_____

_____

_____

How much time did it take you to clearly narrate the introduction (In seconds)?

Introduction visuals

Describe the visual scene or animation happening alongside the narrative. Include an estimate of how long each scene will appear and make sure that, summed together, the scenes equal the time it takes to narrate the introduction.

Visual scene or animation	Length of scene (In seconds)

The need or market pain narrative

Narrate the need or market pain that your project will address. Hit the high points and keep it brief. Statistics are great to include in this section. The description of the need shouldn't be longer than 20 seconds.

_____

_____

_____

_____

_____

_____

_____

How much time did it take you to clearly narrate the need or market pain (In seconds)?

Need or market pain visuals

Describe the visual scene or animation happening alongside the narrative. Include an estimate of how long each scene will appear and make sure that, summed together, the scenes equal the time it takes to narrate the introduction.

Visual scene or animation	Length of scene (In seconds)

Project description and solution narrative

Effectively convey what your project is and why or how it addresses the need, market pain or challenge you described in the previous narrative. Don't just describe your project, tell the audience why it is a compelling solution. In the first section of this guide, we had you identify your project's unique value propositions. Make sure you're including those propositions or differentiators in this narrative. The length of this section will vary depending on the complexity of the project and solution offered. However, as a general guideline, this narrative will be 30-120 seconds long.

_____

_____

_____

_____

_____

_____

_____

How much time did it take you to clearly narrate the project description and solution (In seconds)?

Project description and solution visuals

Describe the visual scene or animation happening alongside the narrative. Include an estimate of how long each scene will appear and make sure that, summed together, the scenes equal the time it takes to narrate the introduction.

Visual scene or animation	Length of scene (In seconds)

Conclusion and "ask" narrative

Now that you've made an introduction, described a need or market pain, described your project and offered a solution, it's time to ask the crowd to contribute. Make sure you tell them specifically what their contribution will help you fund. This narrative should last no longer than 20 seconds.

_____

_____

_____

_____

_____

_____

_____

How much time did it take you to clearly narrate the conclusion and make the "ask"? (In seconds)

Conclusion and ask visuals

Describe the visual scene or animation happening alongside the narrative. Include an estimate of how long each scene will appear and make sure that, summed together, the scenes equal the time it takes to narrate the introduction.

Visual scene or animation	Length of scene (In seconds)